German Cookery

German
Cookery

~~~~~~

by ELIZABETH SCHULER

Edited and Translated by
JOY GARY

CHARLOTTE ADAMS, General Editor
Crown Classic Cookbook Series

CROWN PUBLISHERS, INC.
New York

Published by Crown Publishers, Inc.,
201 East 50th Street, New York, New York 10022.
Member of the Crown Publishing Group.

Random House, Inc. New York, Toronto, London, Sydney, Auckland
www.randomhouse.com

CROWN and colophon are trademarks of Crown Publishers, Inc.

Originally published in German as *Mein Kochbuch*

Printed in the United States of America

Library of Congress Catalog Card Number: 55-7240

ISBN 0-517-50663-7

40 39 38 37 36 35 34 33

FOREWORD

The enormous popularity of this book in Germany is eloquent testimony to its authenticity and dependability. It should be even more welcome here where its audience is twofold. To those already familiar with the many delights of German cooking, *German Cookery* will be happily nostalgic as well as helpful. For those who are not, its refreshingly original suggestions may well revolutionize their menus. So clear and comprehensive is it that both experts and beginners will use it with pleasure and facility.

Old favorites are here: *Lebkuchen, Pfeffernusse, Flammeris, Sauerbraten, Wiener Schnitzel, Pfannkuchen, Schmarren, Spätzle* and *Strudel.* There are new favorites, too, that have established a proven place in present-day Germany. This book is not, however, specialized in any limited sense of that word. It is a complete day-by-day guide to better cooking with the concomitant rewards of better eating. It is inclusive, starting with how not to boil an egg. The gimmick is that you never boil an egg; you soft- or hard-cook it. This accounts for the baffled looks American tourists keep collecting in Europe when they order our inevitable "boiled" eggs. The final chapter on Christmas cakes and candies covers a field in which the Germans traditionally excel. This *Weihnachtsgebäck*, actually, years ago introduced me to German cooking and the German language. I was taken to a Germany bakery, scrubbed and warm and aromatic with deliciously unidentifiable spices. It never occurred to me then that I would one day have a hand in bringing this particular magic into American homes, fresh-baked in American kitchens.

All the ingredients called for in these recipes are available here. The wonderful changes are rung by variations in procedure and intriguing use of familiar ingredients in unexpected ways. The strategic addition of wine, lemon juice and, particularly, lemon peel, gives a sudden Cinderella touch to a basic dish. Patty dough goes on the baking sheet upside down. Juices are often fully absorbed in the cooking process. The approach is always practical and precise, the results epicurean.

v

Quantities have been converted from metric weights to our cups and spoons. In this conversion, as in other phases of this translation, I have been helped by John R. H. Boronow who fortuitously combines mathematical acumen with a first-hand knowledge of German cooking. His assistance has undoubtedly forestalled any such confusion as recently confounded a certain organization. They adopted a foreign child and, wishing to send her some warm clothes, wrote for her measurements. Back came a morass of kilograms and centimeters, accompanied by an alarming effort at translation indicating that their ward weighed 185 pounds, was 4'1" tall, hid behind a 52" bust which tapered to 30" around the hips. A more accurate translation eventually followed, and they were relieved to discover an entirely normal twelve-year-old in their charge. It was the metric system and not the human race that had suffered the sea-change.

Not every potential cook has the culinary equivalent of the gardener's green thumb, nor the enthusiasm, imagination and pride of accomplishment which are the hidden ingredients in all successful cooking. But many a latent talent will come to light with the thoughtful use of this excellent book. May it bring pleasure to your house as it has to ours, where "German recipe" is now synonymous with "extra good."

Joy Gary

CONTENTS

German Cookery

EGG DISHES *(Eierspeisen)*

1. Cooked Eggs *(Gekochte Eier)*

To prevent shells from breaking, place in warm water for 3 minutes before cooking. Cook over slow heat for required time, counting from moment water actually starts to simmer.

For medium-soft eggs— 4 minutes
For hard-cooked eggs—10 minutes

For easier shelling of hard-cooked eggs, dip immediately in cold water.

2. Scrambled Eggs *(Rühreier)*

4 eggs
1 tbls. milk
salt and pepper
chives, chopped
1 tbls. butter
2-3 sliced tomatoes, optional

Beat eggs, milk and seasoning until frothy. Melt butter in skillet over low heat. Pour in mixture, let it set, then stir while it cooks to desired consistency. Before serving, fleck with butter and garnish with finely chopped chives. Gently steamed or lightly fried slices of tomato may be arranged around the platter.
Serves 2.

3. Scrambled Eggs with Ham *(Rühreier mit Schinken)*

4 eggs
1 tbls. milk
salt and pepper
¼ cup cooked ham, diced
1 tbls. butter

Beat eggs, milk and seasoning until frothy. Add ham and mix in. Melt butter in frying pan, pour in mixture, and over slow heat, stir until just set. Serve.
Serves 2.

4. Eggs, Sunny-side up (*Spiegeleier*)

1 tbls. butter
2-4 eggs
salt and pepper

Melt butter in frying pan, remove from heat. Slip in eggs, one after another, keeping yolks whole. Cut away the whites with a fork and stir carefully until they clot. Return, briefly, over strong heat until well done. Sprinkle whites with salt, yolks with pepper, and arrange on a warm platter.
Serves 2.

5. *Spiegeleier* with Ham

2 to 4 slices ham or bacon
1 tsp. butter
2 eggs
salt and pepper

Fry lightly in butter thin slices of ham (or bacon). Break eggs carefully over slices, so as not to break yolks, season, cook until set and serve on a hot plate.
Serves 2.

6. *Spiegeleier* with Cheese

2 slices Swiss cheese
1 tsp. butter
2 eggs
salt and pepper

Place thin slices of Swiss cheese in a buttered skillet. Break eggs over each slice. Cook until set. Or bake in a buttered pan 10 minutes in a moderate (350°) oven. Season and serve.
Serves 2.

7. "Lost" Eggs (*Verlorene, Pochierte, Eier*)

6 cups of water
2 tsp. vinegar
4 eggs
1 tsp. salt (for warm water)

Bring water and vinegar to a boil. Remove from heat and carefully break and slide in eggs, keeping them near surface. Put back on heat and cook 3 to 5 minutes, depending on desired consistency. Remove eggs and place in cold water. Trim ragged edges. Put into warm salt water until ready to serve.

Serves 4.

8. "Lost" Eggs with Bernaise Sauce

6 "Lost" Eggs (No. 7)
Tomato Sauce (No. 284)
    or ketchup

Prepare eggs. Place on a platter and cover, alternately, with red and yellow sauce.

Sauce Bernaise:
3 egg yolks
3 tbls. olive oil
2 tbls. hot water
¼ tbls. vinegar
¼ tsp. salt
few grains cayenne pepper

Beat egg yolks lightly with olive oil, hot water, vinegar, salt and cayenne. Put into a double boiler over hot, not boiling, water and whip until thick. Blend half the sauce with the Tomato Sauce to make the "red sauce."

Serves 6.

9. Tanned Eggs (*Soleier*)

2 qts. water
2 tbls. salt
outer peelings of 2 onions
6 eggs in shell
mustard
mayonnaise, parsley or
    ketchup

Boil water, salt and onion peelings together until solution turns brown. Cook eggs in clear water for 12 minutes, until hard. Crack shells all around but do not remove. Soak eggs in solution for at least 24 hours. Shell and cut in half lengthwise. Remove and dip half-yolks in mustard, replace in whites, and garnish with mayonnaise, parsley or tomato ketchup.

Serves 3.

10. Omelette Soufflé

4 eggs
3 tbls. sugar
juice of ½ lemon
peels of ½ lemon, grated
2 tbls. cornstarch
1½ tbls. butter
confectioner's sugar
¾ tbls. jam or marmalade
⅓ cup cherry brandy

Separate eggs. Stir until frothy the egg yolks, sugar, lemon juice and peels. Add cornstarch. Beat egg whites stiffly and carefully fold in. Butter a pan or mold. Pour mixture into it and bake in a hot (400°) oven until nicely browned, about 12 minutes. Turn out on oiled paper well covered with sugar, spread on jam or marmalade, and fold in two. Place on hot platter. Sprinkle with more sugar. Pour on cherry brandy. Light and serve flaming.
Serves 2.

11. Egg Pudding *(or Soufflé) (Eierauflauf)*

1 cup milk
1 cup sweet cream
2 tbls. butter
2 tbls. flour
4 eggs
1 tsp. salt
pepper

Heat milk and cream. Melt butter. Add flour and, little by little, the milk and cream. Cook in double boiler for 5 minutes. Separate eggs. Beat and add egg yolks to original mixture and stir until thickened. Remove from heat and fold in beaten egg whites and seasoning. Pour into a buttered pan or cupcake forms, set in hot water and bake in moderate (350°) heat for about 45 minutes. Serve with Spanish Sauce, No. 278.
Serves 4.

12. Salzburg "Nockerln" (*Salzburger Nockerln*)

4 eggs
4 tsp. sugar
1 tbls. butter
¼ cup cherry brandy,
    optional

Separate eggs. Stir the egg yolks and sugar until frothy. Beat egg whites until stiff and fold in. Melt butter in a frying pan, and with the pan very hot, brown mixture quickly, or place briefly in a hot oven (425°). "Nockerln" is sometimes cut in strips and served with flaming cherry brandy.
Serves 2.

13. Fluffy Omelet (*Omeletten*)

4 eggs
pinch of salt
1 tbls. butter

Separate eggs. Beat the yolks until frothy. Add salt and beat again. Beat egg whites stiffly and carefully fold in. Heat frying pan, the hotter the better; melt butter in it and pour in the foamy mixture. Rock pan to prevent omelet sticking to the sides. The omelet should be golden brown in less than a second. Loosen from edges, flap over in half, and serve immediately on a hot platter.

Filling:
1 cup diced, cooked mush-
    rooms, or liver, kidneys,
    tomatoes or fruit

If filling is desired, the omelet should be covered with it just before flapping it over. This must be done extremely fast to prevent the omelet from collapsing.
Serves 2.

14. Cheese Omelet *(Käseomeletten)*

2 eggs
7 tbls. flour
nutmeg and salt
milk
¼ cup grated cheese
2 tbls. butter

Mix the eggs, flour and seasoning and stir in enough milk to form a creamy batter. Fold in grated cheese. Heat butter in frying pan and drop in batter a tablespoonful at a time. Cook on both sides until golden brown. Serve with green salad or spinach.
Serves 4.

15. Swiss Eggs *(Eier à la Suisse)*

1 tbls. butter
¼ cup sweet cream
4 eggs
salt, pepper and cayenne
    pepper
¼ cup grated cheese
4 slices of toast
butter for toast and dotting

Melt butter in skillet and add cream. One by one, break eggs into pan (as in No. 4). Sprinkle with seasoning. Just before whites are firm, sprinkle with grated cheese. Complete cooking, dot with butter and serve on buttered toast.
Serves 4.

16. Eggs Victoria *(Eier à la Victoria)*

2 slices of toast
1 tbls. butter
2 chicken livers
2 eggs
½ cup Tomato Sauce
    (No. 284) or ketchup
chives, chopped

Round 2 slices of bread and fry in butter until light golden brown. Remove, add extra butter to the pan if necessary and lightly fry chicken livers. Poach the eggs (see No. 7). On each slice of toast, place first a chicken liver and then a poached egg. Garnish with Tomato Sauce, or ketchup, and chopped chives.
Serves 2.

17. Scrambled Omelet (*Eierhaber*)

2½ cups flour
1 cup milk
3 eggs
pinch of baking powder
2 tbls. butter
salt or sugar and cinnamon

Stir flour, milk, eggs and baking powder into a smooth batter. Melt butter in skillet. Add batter, a spoonful at a time, and brown well on both sides. When done, break up with a fork. Serve on a hot platter. This may be salted before serving and accompanied by vegetables or salads; or sprinkled with cinnamon and sugar to serve with stewed fruits and berries.
Serves 4.

18. Hazelnut Omelet (*Hazelnussomeletten*)

3 tbls. flour
1 cup milk
1 egg, separated
1 tbls. sugar
2 tbls. hazelnuts, grated
salt
2 tbls. butter

Combine flour and milk. Stir in egg yolk, fold in sugar, hazelnuts and stiffly beaten egg white. Add salt to taste. Melt butter and fry omelet golden brown on both sides. Serve with stewed fruits or berries.
Serves 2.

SANDWICHES AND CANAPÉS
(Sandwiches und Canapés)

19. Russian Herring Canapés
(*Russische Heringsbrötchen*)

½ cup fillets of herring
½ cup chopped apples
¼ cup mayonnaise
toast
1 hard-cooked egg, chopped
cucumber pickle

Cut smoked or pickled herring in small pieces. Mix with thinly sliced tart apples. Bind with mayonnaise. Spread on toast squares and garnish with chopped eggs and bits of cucumber pickle.
Makes about 16-18.

20. Goose Liver Canapés *(Gänsleberbrötchen)*

1 goose liver
3 tbls. butter
1 truffle (save a little for garnish)
1 shallot
1 tbls. Madeira
salt and pepper
toast or French bread
truffle
aspic (No. 293)

Sauté liver in 1 tablespoon of the butter. Cool and chop. Cream remaining butter and mix in finely chopped liver, truffle and shallot. Add Madeira and seasonings to taste and mix well. Heap mixture on squares of toast or pieces of French bread. Garnish each piece with a touch of truffle and a dot of aspic.
Makes about 8.

21. Chili Spread *(Chilalyaufstrich)*

2 tbls. finely chopped red or green peppers
2 tbls. onion, minced
1 tbls. butter
½ cup Tomato Sauce (No. 284) or ketchup
¾ lb. mild cheese
salt and pepper
2 tbls. milk
1 egg yolk
toast

Mix pepper and onion with butter and heat together for 3 minutes. Add Tomato Sauce and continue cooking for 5 more minutes. Dice cheese and add to mixture. Season to taste. Cook until cheese melts. Fold in the milk and lightly beaten egg yolk. Mixture may be spread, hot, on thin pieces of toast or used, cold, as a sandwich filling.
Makes about 24 canapés or 6 sandwiches.

22. Egg Paste Canapés with Anchovy *(Eiercremebrötchen mit Sardellen)*

3 hard-cooked eggs
2 tbls. butter
1 tbls. sweet cream
salt and pepper
toast or French bread
flat anchovy fillets
cucumbers or tomatoes
parsley

Mash eggs through strainer. Cream butter and add cream, seasoning and the eggs. Spread generously on squares of toast or pieces of French bread and garnish with a criss-cross of anchovies. Or use on top of sliced cucumbers or tomatoes. Decorate with finely chopped parsley.
Makes about 10-12.

23. Spanish Canapés (*Spanische Sandwiches*)

2 anchovy fillets
2 pickles
1 tsp. parsley, chopped
2 tbls. capers
2 hard-cooked eggs
1 tsp. mustard
2 tbls. olive oil
2 tbls. vinegar
salt and paprika
dark bread and butter

Chop anchovies, pickles, parsley, capers and egg yolks. Add mustard, olive oil, vinegar and blend to a paste. Season with salt and paprika. Slice bread thinly and spread, thinly, with butter. Cut off crusts and cut into squares or other desired shapes. Top with the mixture and garnish with chopped egg white.
Makes about 10-12.

24. Lobster Canapés I (*Hummersandwiches*)

1 cup lobster meat
2 hard-cooked egg yolks
2 tbls. butter
½ tsp. mustard, prepared
salt and pepper
1 bouillon cube or soup
    stock
buttered toast

Chop lobster meat and egg yolks and put through food mill. Cream butter. Add mustard, seasoning and enough soup stock or diluted bouillon cubes to moisten. Mix well with lobster and egg. Spread on buttered squares of toast.
Makes 12-16.

25. Lobster Canapés II (*Hummercanapés*)

2 tbls. butter
2 tbls. sweet cream
1 cup lobster meat
1 cooked egg yolk
½ tsp. salt
¼ tsp. mustard
dash cayenne
¼ tsp. beef extract
toast
2 hard-cooked eggs, sliced

Melt butter and add cream. Chop lobster meat very fine. Chop and add an equal amount of hard-cooked egg and put through a food mill. Soften with melted butter and cream. Season well. Spread on toast rounds and garnish with slices of hard-cooked eggs.
Makes about 12-16.

26. Dream Sandwiches *(Traumsandwiches)*

10 slices day-old bread
½ lb. mild cheese, sliced thin
salt and pepper
butter

Slice day-old bread ½ inch thick. Cut in rectangular strips ⅔ inches wide. Top with cheese, sprinkle with salt and pepper and fold over into squares. Fry lightly on both sides in butter.

27. Sardine Canapés *(Sardinencanapés)*

1 can sardines
2 tbls. butter
¼ tsp. Worcestershire sauce
pepper
toast
stuffed olives
whites of hard-cooked eggs

Bone and mash sardines. Cream butter, season with Worcestershire sauce and freshly ground pepper. Mix with sardines and spread on toast squares. Garnish with slices of stuffed olives and chopped egg whites.
Makes about 12-16.

28. Cheese and Olive Canapés *(Käse und Olivencanapés)*

day-old bread
¼ cup butter
6 ozs. cream cheese
salt
olives
red or green peppers

Slice day-old bread and trim into ovals ½ inch thick. Cream butter and mix well with cream cheese. Season, and spread on bread. Garnish with finely chopped olives and small pieces of red or green peppers.
Makes 18-20.

29. Piquant Tarts *(Torteletten pikant)*

Dough:
1¾ cups flour
2 egg yolks
½ cup grated Parmesan
 cheese
5-7 tbls. butter
pinch of salt
egg whites for brushing

Mix all dough ingredients and quickly knead smooth. Roll out ¼ inch thick and cut with biscuit cutter. Brush with egg white. Build up rounds with a rim of leftover dough to form tarts. Bake at medium (350°) heat for about 15 minutes, or until golden-brown. Cool, and then fill with various mixtures; in each case creaming 1 tablespoon butter and blending in other ingredients:

Fillings (for each tart):
(a)
1 tsp. ketchup
salt and pepper
chopped tomato
(b)
1 tsp. salmon
1 slice egg

(c)
1 tsp. anchovy paste
anchovy strips
(d)
1 tsp. cheese
radish slice

(a) butter, ketchup, salt and pepper, garnished with chopped tomato.

(b) butter, salmon paste or flaked salmon garnished with chopped, hard-cooked egg.

(c) butter, anchovy paste, garnished with strips of anchovy.

(d) butter, crumbled Roquefort, Bleu or Gorgonzola cheese, garnished with sliced radish.

Serves 4.

30. Cheese Crackers *(Käsecrackers)*

½ lb. Cheddar cheese
2 tbls. butter
3 tbls. sherry
2 tbls. cream
1 tsp. mustard
salt and pepper
crackers

Cut up cheese and put through moistened meat grinder. Lightly cream the butter. Mix in sherry, cream and seasoning and add to cheese. Spread with a pastry-decorator on unsweetened crackers. Serve with tea, punch or wine.

Serves 4.

31. Stuffed Dark Bread *(Gefülltes Kapselbrot)*

1 square loaf dark bread
2 hard-cooked eggs
½ cup anchovies
6-8 tbls. butter
1 cup chopped ox tongue or
   1 cup chopped ham
½ cup Swiss cheese
1 tbls. capers
1 tbls. mustard
salt and pepper
aspic (No. 293)
1 tomato, sliced
parsley

Remove crusts from bread and from the top, scoop out most of the insides. Chop eggs finely. Put anchovies through a strainer. Cream butter. Mix all together with the tongue or ham, cheese, capers and seasoning. Stuff into hollow loaf and chill in refrigerator. To serve, slice, and garnish with aspic, slices of tomato and parsley.

Serves 4.

32. Ham and Egg Mayonnaise *(Mayonnaise-Eierbrötchen)*

2 eggs
3 slices cooked ham
mayonnaise
2 pieces buttered toast

Prepare poached eggs (see No. 7). Let cool. Chop finely one slice of ham and mix with cold eggs and mayonnaise. Place a slice of ham on each of two pieces of buttered toast, or bread fried in butter. Top with the egg-mayonnaise.

Serves 2.

33. Herring on Toast *(Heringstoast)*

1 herring, boned and salted
1 slice bacon, fried
1 hard-cooked egg
1 small onion, minced
1 tbls. olive oil
toast, buttered
capers
cucumber slices

Soak boned, salted herring in water. Remove and chop finely together with bacon, egg and onion. Blend in oil. Spread mixture on two pieces of buttered toast and garnish with capers and slices of cucumber.

Serves 2.

34. Tomato Spread *(Tomatenaufstrich)*

2 tbls. butter
2 tbls. flour
¼ cup cream
½ cup Tomato Sauce
   (No. 284) or ketchup
⅛ tsp. baking powder
2 eggs
2 cups cheese
salt, pepper and mustard
toast

Over moderate heat, or in a double boiler, melt butter and mix flour in smoothly. Add cream little by little. As mixture begins to thicken, fold in sauce mixed with baking powder. Lightly beat eggs, cheese and seasoning, and add. When cheese is entirely melted, pour entire mixture over toast and serve.

Serves 4.

APPETIZERS *(Vorspeisen)*

35. Roasted Oysters *(Geröstete Austern)*

2 doz. oysters
salt, pepper and other
   desired seasoning

Wash oysters. Place in pan and bake in hot oven (400°) until shells open. Remove top shell. Season to taste and serve in shell.

Serves 2.

36. Oyster Cocktail *(Austerncocktail)*

10 oysters
2 tbls. ketchup
1 tbls. grated horseradish
¼ tsp. Worcestershire sauce
¼ tsp. Tabasco sauce
1 tsp. lemon juice
pinch of salt
2 slices of lemon

Shuck oysters and dip in clear water to remove any grit. Blend together all other ingredients to make a sauce. Put five oysters in each tall glass and pour sauce over them. Garnish with a slice of lemon. Cool and serve.

Instead of oysters, sardines, tuna or salmon may be used.

Serves 2.

37. Lobster Mayonnaise (*Hummermayonnaise*)

1 lobster
juice of 1 lemon
salt and pepper
1 cup mayonnaise
1 hard-cooked egg, sliced
½ can anchovy fillets
6 capers
1 sliced tomato

Remove cooked lobster (see No. 103) from shell. Sprinkle chunks with lemon juice, salt and pepper. Arrange neatly on a glass salad plate between mounds of mayonnaise. Pour remaining mayonnaise over lobster pieces and serve garnished with sliced hard-cooked eggs, anchovies, capers and sliced tomato.

This same recipe may be used for salmon, crabmeat, and most varieties of cooked or canned fish.

Serves 4.

38. Tomatoes Nana (*Tomaten Nana*)

4 large tomatoes
1 cup cooked chicken
½ cup walnuts
salt and pepper
½ cup cream
½ cup mayonnaise
lettuce

Scald, peel, and partially hollow out tomatoes. Chop chicken and nuts finely; add salt, pepper and cream. Mix well, stuff into tomato shells and garnish with mayonnaise. Serve cold, with lettuce, on a salad plate.

Serves 4.

39. Tomatoes Lucullus (*Tomaten Lukullus*)

2 large, or 4 small tomatoes
1 hard-cooked egg
1 cup cooked chicken
1 stick celery
2 anchovies
4 olives
4 capers
¼ cup mixed nuts
½ cup mayonnaise
1 tbls. lemon juice
lettuce

Wash and polish tomatoes. Cut off a little of the top and save. Hollow out tomatoes. Chop up egg, chicken, celery, anchovies, olives, capers and nuts. Moisten with mayonnaise, and season with salt and pepper. Sprinkle with lemon juice and fill tomato shells. Replace top and serve with lettuce on salad plates.

Serves 2.

40. **Smorgasbord** *(Schwedische Platte)*

Arrange on a partitioned platter, or in individual dishes, on a platter, a variety of specialties, for example: any kind of vegetable salad, Mushroom Salad (No. 253), Lobster Mayonnaise (No. 37), Ox Tongue Salad (No. 263), Egg Salad (No. 43), tuna in oil, sardines in oil, smoked herring, salmon, etc., sliced salami, ham, Goose Liver Paté (No. 42), Chicken Salad (No. 261), stuffed eggs, Tomatoes Nana (No. 38). Garnish with olives, small pickles, sliced lemon and sprigs of parsley. Serve with bread and butter.

41. **Salmon Cones with Cream** *(Lachstüten mit Rahm)*

2 tbls. horseradish
1 tbls. vinegar
salt and pinch of sugar
gelatine
½ cup whipping cream
6 slices smoked salmon

Mix grated horseradish, vinegar, salt and sugar. Dissolve gelatine and add. Fold in whipping cream. Roll salmon slices into cones and fill with mixture. Put in refrigerator to harden.
Serves 2.

42. **Hungarian Goose Liver Paté** *(Gänseleberpastete, Ungarisch)*

1 truffle
1 large goose liver
3 tbls. Madeira wine or milk
8 tbls. goose fat
1 onion
salt and pepper

Slice a truffle and lard a large, fat goose liver with it. Be very careful. Let it soak briefly in Madeira or milk. Brown onion in goose fat, add liver and cook until well done, about 15 minutes. Remove liver and season well. Place in deep china bowl, pour fat over it through a fine strainer. Let cool and serve.
Serves 2-3.

43. Egg Salad *(Eiersalat)*

5 eggs
½ cup cream
4 tbls. oil
2 tbls. mustard
1 tbls. lemon juice
salt and pepper
salad spices to taste
pinch of sugar
hearts of lettuce
cucumber and tomato slices

Cook eggs for 15 minutes, chill and peel. Remove yolk from one egg and mash. Slice other eggs thinly. Mix mashed yolk well with cream, oil, mustard and lemon juice, salt, pepper and other desired spices, and sugar, to make a sauce. Arrange sliced eggs on platter and pour sauce over them. Garnish with hearts of lettuce and slices of cucumber and tomato. Chill and serve.
Serves 4.

44. Beef Salad *(Feiner Rindfleischsalat)*

Marinade:
1 tbls. mustard
4 tbls. beef stock
2 tbls. vinegar
2 tbls. oil
salt and pepper

1 lb. well-cooked beef
1 hard-cooked egg
1 cooked potato
1 small onion
5 small pickled cucumbers
parsley

Mix marinade ingredients well. Dice all other ingredients finely, or cut in slices or strips. Mix into marinade, decorate with parsley. Chill and serve.
Serves 3.

45. Fish Salad with Tomato Sauce
(*Fischsalat mit Tomatenmark*)

2¼ lbs. fillet of fish
½ cup lemon juice
1 tbls. salt
1 raw egg
½ cup flour
fat or oil

Marinade:
2 tbls. vinegar
4 tbls. oil
1 tbls. mustard
2 tbls. Tomato Sauce
(No. 284) or ketchup
salt and pepper

Sprinkle fillets of fish with lemon juice and salt and let stand 10 minutes. Dip into beaten egg and flour and fry in hot fat. Cool and chop. Chill thoroughly. Blend marinade ingredients well and pour over fish. Garnish with mayonnaise. Serves 4.

46. Celery with Roquefort Cheese
(*Bleichsellerie mit Roquefortkäse*)

1 stalk of celery
4 tbls. butter
8 tbls. Roquefort cheese
salt and paprika

Wash and scrape celery and cut in 2-inch lengths. Cream butter and mix well with cheese. Add salt and paprika to taste. Spread mixture in hollow of celery and serve on ice. Serves 4.

47. Cheese "Truffles" (*Käsetrüffel*)

3 tbls. butter
1 pkg. cream cheese
1 tsp. sweet or sour cream
1 tsp. sugar
grated dark pumpernickel

Cream butter. Mash cream cheese and add cream and sugar. Mix well with butter to form thick paste. Chill. Form into balls and roll in grated pumpernickel. Place resulting "truffles" in paper cups, of suitable size, if desired, and chill well before serving. Serves 2.

48. Parmesan Patties (*Käsecreme*)

2 cups milk
2 egg yolks
1 cup Parmesan, grated
1 tbls. cornstarch
1 tsp. paprika
pinch of cinnamon
pinch of salt
parsley, olive or pimento

To the milk add egg yolks, Parmesan, cornstarch and seasoning and mix well. Heat thoroughly over low heat, stirring constantly until thick. Pour into small greased molds or custard cups and chill. To serve, turn out and decorate as desired, with a sprig of parsley, a little chopped olive or pimento.
Serves 4.

SOUPS, HOT AND COLD
(*Suppen und Kaltschalen*)

49. Strong Beef Broth (*Kraftbrühe*)

4½ lbs. beef chuck
1 soup bone
soup greens
salt
1 gallon water

Start beef, bones, soup greens and salt in cold water and simmer for approximately 4 hours. Remove foam as it appears on the surface and, to replace water lost by evaporation, add a cup of cold water about every half-hour. When done, strain. To serve cold, skim off fat first.
Serves 6-8.

50. Oatmeal Soup (*Haferflockensuppe*)

1 qt. water or stock
1 tsp. salt
½ cup oatmeal
2 egg yolks
1 cup cream or
    4 tbls. butter

Cook raw oatmeal in salted water or seasoned stock for 5 to 10 minutes. Beat egg yolks and beat quickly into soup. Add either cream or butter and heat, but *do not boil*.
Serves 4.

51. Brain Soup (*Hirnsuppe*)

1 calf's brain
2 tbls. butter
flour
1 qt. beef stock
1 egg yolk
1 cup cream

To wash brain clear of blood, soak in cold water, renewing water several times. Skin and chop fine. Melt butter in pan, add brain, sprinkle with flour, and sauté 10 minutes. Add beef stock and simmer 20 minutes. Just before serving, stir in egg yolk and cream.
Serves 4-6.

52. Asparagus Soup (*Spargelsuppe*)

1 lb. asparagus
1 qt. water, salted slightly
4 tbls. flour
4 tbls. butter
1 egg yolk
2 tbls. cream

Clean the asparagus and cut into inch-long pieces. Cook until tender in slightly salted water. Make white sauce by stirring flour into melted butter, adding dashes of asparagus water until flour is completely dissolved. Add to soup and thicken with beaten egg yolk and cream.
Serves 4.

53. Cauliflower Soup (*Blumenkohlsuppe*)

1 head cauliflower
1 qt. water, salted
4 tbls. butter
4 tbls. flour
1 egg yolk
2 tbls. cream
nutmeg to taste

Clean cauliflower, pluck apart into "bouquets" and soak for one hour in cold salt water. Cook in one quart of salted water, Melt butter, and flour, and half a cup of cooking water and stir until completely dissolved. Add to soup and bring to a boil once more. Thicken with beaten egg yolk and cream. Season with nutmeg. Return bouquets and serve.
Serves 4.

54. Cream of Vegetable Soup *(Gemüsecremesuppe)*

1 lb. vegetables
1 qt. water, salted slightly
3 tbls. butter
4 tbls. flour
salt
2 tbls. cream
parsley, chopped

Clean and chop up any desired selection of fresh vegetables. Cook until tender in one quart of slightly salted water. Put vegetables through strainer, reserving liquid. Melt butter, blend in flour and gradually add one cup of cooking water, stirring over low heat until completely dissolved. Combine with original cooking water and vegetables. Stir and season. Bring to boil and enrich with cream. Serve garnished with parsley.
Serves 4.

55. Green Potato Soup *(Grüne Kartoffelsuppe)*

1 lb. raw potatoes
1-2 tomatoes
1 yellow turnip
1 piece of celery
1 onion
2 tbls. butter
1 tbls. flour
1½ qts. water or stock
½ tsp. salt
1-2 tbls. sour cream
parsley
2 slices toasted dark bread

Dice potatoes and vegetables. Melt butter and heat potatoes and vegetables in it. *Do not brown.* Sprinkle with flour. Add water or beef stock and salt. Cook thoroughly 25 to 35 minutes. Before serving enrich with cream and garnish with parsley. Cube toast to make croutons and sprinkle over top.
Serves 4-6.

56. Lentil, Pea or Bean Soup
(*Linsen, Erbsen, Bohnensuppe*)

¼ lb. legumes
salt
1-2 tbls. butter or fat
4 tbls. flour
2 strips of bacon or Vienna
    sausage or toasted bread
marjoram or
    vinegar or
    garlic

Soak legumes overnight in cold water. Drain, cover with 2 quarts salted water and cook until tender, about 2 hours. Put legumes through a strainer. Melt butter, add flour and 1 cup of cooking water and stir, over low heat, to smooth consistency. Add to strained legumes. Chop bacon finely, fry it lightly, and add to soup. Or cut Vienna sausage into it. Season pea soup with a little marjoram; lentil soup with a little vinegar; bean soup with a trace of garlic, each, to taste. Croutons of toast may be added before serving. Serves 4-6.

57. Dark Bread Soup (*Schwarzbrotsuppe*)

1 lb. dark bread
2 qts. water
¼ tsp. caraway seeds
salt
1 small onion
1 tbls. fat
2 bouillon cubes or cream

Soak dark bread in water, bring to a boil, remove and strain. Bring to a boil again, if necessary adding more water. Season. Chop an onion finely and brown in fat, and add. Enrich, if desired, with bouillon cubes or cream. Serves 4-6.

58. Beer Soup (*Biersuppe*)

2 bottles beer
2 tbls. flour
1 tbls. sugar
1 tbls. butter
¼ lemon; juice and chopped
    peels
¼ tsp. cinnamon
1-2 eggs, beaten

Open beer and let it get flat, at least 2 hours. Brown the flour and sugar in melted butter. Add beer, lemon juice, lemon peels and cinnamon and cook. Stir in beaten eggs. Serve hot or chilled. Diced dark toast may be added. Serves 4.

59. Buttermilk Soup *(Buttermilchsuppe)*

1 lb. raw potatoes
salted water
1 tbls. flour
1 qt. buttermilk
3 strips bacon
1 onion
salt and pepper

Peel and chop potatoes and cook until tender in salted water. Drain. Mix flour and buttermilk and bring to a boil. Chop bacon and onion finely and brown. Combine, season, and serve.
Serves 4.

60. Dutch Oyster Soup
(Amsterdamer Austernsuppe)

3 cups oysters
1 qt. water
3 tbls. flour
3 tbls. butter
salt, paprika and celery salt
¼ cup cream

Chop up oysters and cook about 1 minute in their own liquid. Force through strainer or cheesecloth. Add one quart of water. Brown flour in butter and slowly stir in oyster broth. Cook over low heat for 30 minutes. Season with salt, paprika and celery salt. Just before serving, stir in cream.
Serves 4.

61. Cold Fruit Soup—
Apple, Cherry, Rhubarb, Gooseberry
(Apfel, Kirsch, Rhabarber,
Stachelbeerkaltschale)

1 lb. any fruit
2 qts. water
1 tbls. cornstarch or
    4 tbls. tapioca
2 tbls. sugar
¼ lemon, juice and chopped
    peels
¼ cup white wine, optional

Cook fruits in two quarts of water until soft. Drain, reserving liquid. Put through a fine strainer. Replace pulp in liquid and cook briefly again. Dissolve cornstarch (or tapioca) in ½ cup water or fruit juice and add to liquid. If tapioca is used, cook until it is transparent. Flavor with sugar and lemon to taste. White wine may be added. Garnish with cut fruit or whole berries; chill and serve cold.
Serves 4-6.

62. Cold Wine Soup (*Weinkaltschale*)

3 cups water
5 tbls. raisins
5 tbls. semolina
1 cup water
2 egg yolks
2 tbls. sugar
1 cup white wine
juice of ½ lemon
2 egg whites
5 tbls. sugar
dash of cinnamon

Bring to a boil 3 cups of water and raisins. Mix semolina with one cup of water. Add to raisins and water and stir well. Cook for 20 minutes. Blend egg yolks, sugar, wine and lemon juice and stir into soup. Keep on low heat for 4 minutes. Cool and place in refrigerator. Beat egg whites with a little sugar, until stiff. Then drop small floats of this into soup (like croutons). Serve cold, with cinnamon and sugar sprinkled on top. Serves 4.

SOUP GARNISHES (*Suppeneinlagen*)

63. Butter Balls (*Butterklösschen*)

3 tbls. butter
2 egg yolks
4 tbls. flour
salt and nutmeg to taste

Cream butter. Add, alternately, small amounts of egg yolks and flour, season, and stir to a froth. Let mixture stand one hour. Measure teaspoon-size lumps into soup (or stock) and cook over slow heat until balls float on the surface. Serves 4.

64. Farina Dumplings (*Griessklösschen*)

½ cup milk
2 tbls. butter
salt and nutmeg
4 tbls. farina
2 eggs

Bring the milk, butter and seasoning to a boil. Sprinkle in farina and form into a lump. Remove from heat and, singly, mix in eggs. Cool. Cut into small dumplings. Place in boiling soup stock until dumplings rise to the surface. Serves 4.

65. Flour Dumplings *(Schwemmklösschen)*

¼ cup milk
2 tbls. butter
salt and nutmeg
6 tbls. flour
2 eggs

Bring the milk, butter and seasoning to a boil. Sprinkle in flour and form into a loaf. Let cool; then, singly, mix in eggs. From a spoon, slip dumplings into boiling soup stock and cook 4 to 6 minutes. Serves 4.

66. Bread Dumplings *(Weckklösschen)*

2 pieces stale bread
1 tbls. butter
parsley, salt and nutmeg
1 egg

Grate bread, or cut in very small pieces, and dampen with hot soup stock. Cream butter and add seasoning, egg and bread crumbs. Blend well. Form balls, drop into boiling soup stock. Cut down heat and let stay for 5 minutes. Serves 4.

67. Marrow Balls *(Markklösschen)*

3 ozs. beef marrow
2 rolls
4 tbls. milk
2 eggs
1 tbls. flour
salt, pepper and nutmeg

Melt marrow over low heat. Soak rolls in milk and squeeze dry. Mix together all ingredients and shape into dumplings. Place in soup stock and let simmer until they float to the surface. Serves 4.

68. Liver Dumplings (*Leberklösschen*)

¼ lb. calf's liver
3 small rolls
1 onion
parsley
2 tbls. butter
5 tbls. flour
2 eggs
salt, nutmeg and marjoram

Grind liver. Break up rolls, soak in water and pluck apart. Chop onion and parsley finely and blend with butter. Combine all ingredients. With a spoon, drop little balls into boiling soup stock and cook for 10 minutes.
Serves 4.

69. Egg Cubes (*Eierstich*)

butter (for greasing)
1 egg yolk
1 whole egg
¼ cup milk
salt and nutmeg

Butter top pan of double boiler. Beat together all ingredients and pour into greased pan. Cover, heat for about 20 minutes, until mixture is firm. Turn out, cool and cut into cubes.
Serves 4.

70. Butter Biscuit (*Butterbiskuit*)

4 tbls. butter
2-3 eggs, separated
6 tbls. flour
1 tsp. parsley
salt or nutmeg

Cream butter and to it add, alternately, small quantities of egg yolks and flour. Beat egg whites until stiff. Fold into mixture and add parsley and seasoning. Butter cake pan. Pour in mixture and bake in moderate (350°) oven until golden brown. Cool, cut in cubes and drop in soup to serve.
Serves 4.

71. Small Flat Cakes (Flädle)

1¼ cups flour
1 cup milk
1 whole egg
salt, nutmeg to taste
bacon rind or fat for
    greasing

Stir flour, milk, egg and seasoning to a smooth batter. Rub a griddle with bacon or melt a little fat in it and heat well. Ladle spoonfuls of batter onto griddle and let spread thinly. Fry until golden brown on both sides. When cool, cut into thin strips. Serve in hot soup, garnished with parsley or chives.

Serves 4.

72. Homemade Soup Noodles (Nudeln)

1 egg
½ cup water, iced
1 cup flour

Beat egg and water. Gradually add flour until a firm dough is formed. Strew flour on a bread board, turn out dough and knead until very pliable. The dough, when cut, should have small bubbles in it. Roll out to desired thickness and let stand to dry out. Roll up and cut into fine ribbons. Spread out for further drying. Toss into soup stock and boil for not over 5 minutes.

Serves 4.

73. Noodles "Riebele"

1 egg
½ cup water, iced
1¼ cups flour

Prepare dough as in No. 72. Instead of cutting in ribbons, grate through coarse part of cheese-grater, rubbing dough downward only. Let dry thoroughly. Add to soup stock and boil for not over 5 minutes.

Serves 4.

74. Sponge Soup Noodles (*Schwammnudeln*)

2 eggs, separated
2 tsp. milk
1 cup flour
salt and nutmeg

Beat egg whites until stiff. Carefully fold in milk, egg yolks, flour and seasoning. Pour entire mixture into soup stock and, without stirring, let it jell. Cook over slow heat for 5 minutes. To serve, cut the custard-like substance into small cubes.

Serves 4.

FISH *(Fische)*

75. Blue Trout (*Forellen, blau*)

4 trout
1 tbls. vinegar and water
2½ qts. water
1 cup vinegar
salt
lemon wedges
parsley

For best results trout should be fresh-caught, and cleaned under water, holding by head so that sheen is not lost. It is this sheen that gives the fish its blue color. Place fish on a moistened platter. Mix the tablespoon of vinegar and water (half and half) and heat. Sprinkle over fish and let stand 5 minutes. Mix water, vinegar and salt and cook trout in mixture over low heat, for 10 to 15 minutes. Serve on hot platter, or in folded napkin. Garnish with parsley and lemon wedges. Serve with Salted Potatoes (No. 199) and fresh or melted butter or Sauce Bernaise (No. 273).

Serves 4.

76. Trout in White Wine *(Forellen in Weisswein)*

4 trout
4 tomatoes
1 banana
estragon
4 shallots
½ cup white wine
salt and pepper
1 cup Hollandaise Sauce
(No. 272)

Clean fish and put in a saucepan. Surround with tomatoes, quartered, and bananas, finely sliced, a little estragon, and chopped shallots. Pour wine over this, season and cook slowly over moderate heat. When half done (about 6 minutes) turn fish over and finish cooking. Carefully remove fish, skin and keep hot until ready to serve. Let sauce boil down somewhat. Prepare Hollandaise Sauce and blend in over moderate heat. Pour over fish to serve.

Serves 4.

77. Jellied Trout *(Gesulzte Forellen)*

4 small trout
6 cups water
1 cup vinegar
salt and peppercorns
½ onion, chopped
1 cup white wine
5 envelopes gelatine, dissolved
2 egg whites
1 lemon
tomatoes
crab or lobster tails
parsley
Remoulade Sauce (No. 279)

Prepare trout (see No. 75) and let cool in steeping solution of water, vinegar, salt, peppercorns and chopped onion. Remove. Skim fat from solution and reheat. Add wine and dissolved gelatine. Beat egg whites and add, gently stirring in while boiling. Remove from heat and let stand in warm place until egg whites have solidified and liquid appears clear. Filter liquid through cloth, repeating if necessary, and pour one-third of liquid into mold of suitable size. Chill and when firm lay fish on top. Pour in remaining liquid and chill again until firm. The idea is to have fish "float" in the middle of the jelly. To remove, loosen around edges with thin knife and turn out on a platter. Decorate with slices of lemon, tomatoes, crab or lobster tails, and parsley. Serve with Remoulade Sauce.

Serves 4.

78. Blue Eel (*Aal, blau*)

2½ lbs. eel
1 cup vinegar
½ gal. water
1 small onion, chopped
1 tbls. salt
1 bay leaf
peppercorns and thyme
1 lemon
parsley

Cut up eel in bite-size pieces. Clean and dry. Heat vinegar, pour over eel and let stand 5 minutes. Add boiling water, chopped onion and seasoning. Soak for 25 minutes. Serve on a hot platter, garnished with parsley and lemon wedges or slices. Serve with Remoulade Sauce (No. 279) or Caper Sauce (No. 282), Potato Salad (No. 258) or Cucumber Salad (No. 244).

Serves 4-5.

79. Grilled Eel (*Aal nach Trentiner Art*)

2½ lbs. eel
olive oil
lemon juice
marjoram
salt and pepper
Parmesan cheese, grated

Skin eel and cut in 2-inch slices. Sprinkle with oil and lemon juice; add seasoning to taste. Spear on large toothpicks. Grill under high heat for 15 minutes, until golden-brown. To serve sprinkle with salt and grated Parmesan cheese.
Serves 4.

80. Sole in White Wine (*Seezunge in Weisswein*)

1 lb. sole
2 tbls. butter
1 cup sauterne or any
    white wine
1 tbls. flour
salt and pepper
1 tsp. lemon juice

Detach skin at tail and pull off whole. Trim off head and tail. Rinse and sprinkle with salt. Melt butter, add wine and fish and steam until tender, about 20 minutes. Remove and keep hot. To the wine and butter sauce, add flour and extra butter and bring to a boil. Season and sprinkle with lemon juice. For a thicker sauce, add beaten egg yolk. Pour over fish to serve. Serve with Salted Potatoes (No. 199).
Serves 2.

81. Fillets of Sole in Butter *(Seezunge in Butter)*

3 tbls. butter
salt and pepper
2 fillets of sole
3 more tbls. butter
1 lemon
parsley

Melt butter, add seasoning and brown fillets lightly. Place on hot platter. Add extra butter to pan, and when melted, without further heating, pour over fillets. Garnish with parsley and thin slices of seeded lemon. Serve with Salted Potatoes (No. 199).
Serves 2.

82. Fried Sole *(Seezunge, gebacken—Soles frites)*

2¼ lbs. fillet of sole
salt and pepper
1 whole egg, beaten
3 tbls. flour
bread crumbs
fat
lemon wedges
parsley

Cut sole in long, thin, diagonal strips. Rub in salt and pepper. Dip in beaten egg. Tumble in flour. Dip again in egg and then in bread crumbs, to achieve a crunchy crust. Fry in deep fat until brown. Garnish with lemon wedges and parsley. Serve with Potato Salad (No. 199) and Remoulade Sauce (No. 279).
Serves 3-4.

83. Grilled Salmon *(Lachs, gegrillt)*

2½ lbs. salmon
    (center cut)
lemon juice
olive oil
1 large onion, sliced
salt and pepper

Slice salmon in finger-width slices. Sprinkle with lemon juice and olive oil. Cover with sliced onion and let stand one hour. Remove onions, and grill fish under moderate heat, turning as it browns for 20 minutes. Add seasoning to taste. Serve with Salted Potatoes (No. 199), raw sliced cucumbers and Sauce Bernaise (No. 273).
Serves 4.

84. Boiled Salmon (*Salm*)

2¼ lbs. salmon
2 qts. water
⅓ cup white wine
2 tbls. vinegar
1 small onion, peeled
½ bay leaf
1 clove
1 lemon, sliced
peppercorns
salt and pepper
lemon slices
parsley

Bring all ingredients (except salmon) to a boil and remove from heat. Clean fish and put in brew. Cover and let simmer over low heat for 30 minutes. Drain. Garnish with lemon slices and parsley. Serve on hot platter. Serve with new parsley potatoes and Hollandaise Sauce (No. 272).

Serves 4.

85. Boiled Flounder (*Steinbutt, gekocht*)

2-3 lbs. flounder
lemon juice
2 qts. water
spices to taste
salt and pepper
1 onion
mixed soup vegetables—
    1 cup or more
½ cup sauterne

Have fish split and cleaned. Sprinkle thoroughly inside and out with salt. Wash off salt and dry fish. Sprinkle with lemon juice and place flesh side up in a long pan. Cover with cold water, add spices, seasonings, onion, soup vegetables and sauterne. Bring to a boil, then let simmer on low heat 30 to 40 minutes. Serve flesh-side up on hot platter. Serve with Salted Potatoes (No. 199), Hollandaise Sauce (No. 272) or Brown Butter (No. 295).

Serves 4-6.

86. Lake Trout (*Gebratene Forellen*)
Also can be used for Lake Salmon (Felchen)

2 lake trout
juice of ½ lemon
3 tbls. flour
3 tbls. butter
parsley
salt and pepper
½ lemon, sliced

Clean trout. Sprinkle with lemon juice and roll in flour. Melt butter in skillet and fry trout about 5 minutes on each side. Keep hot until ready to serve. For the sauce use original butter or, if it is too brown, melt fresh butter and brown in it chopped parsley, seasoning and more lemon juice. Pour over trout. Garnish with lemon slices. Serve with Salted Potatoes (No. 199).

Serves 2.

87. Pike in Sour Cream *(Hecht in sauren Rahm)*

3 lbs. pike or perch
7 tbls. butter
2 cups white wine
3 anchovies
4 slices lemon, peeled
    and seeded
4 tbls. bread crumbs
salt and pepper
1 cup sour cream

Clean fish thoroughly and cut in fair-sized portions. Melt butter, add wine, chopped anchovies, lemon slices, bread crumbs and seasoning. Simmer fish in this for about 20 minutes over low heat. Add cream, bring to a boil, season further if desired. (The same recipe can be used for perch.) Serve with boiled potatoes or buttered rice.
Serves 5-6.

88. Grilled Carp *(Karpfen, gegrillt)*

1 carp, about 3 lbs.
lemon juice
salt

Clean carp and cut in 6 pieces. Sprinkle with lemon juice. Broil, turning once, for 25 minutes. Season with salt and serve on a hot plate.
Serves 6.

89. Christmas Carp *(Karpfen polnisch)*

¼ cup cherries
2½ lbs. carp
butter
1 stalk celery
1 onion
1 yellow turnip
parsley root
2 cloves
peppercorns
1 bay leaf
salt and pepper
1 cup water
1 bottle beer
2″ square piece of
    gingerbread
½ lemon peel
½ cup of almonds
¼ cup raisins
sugar

Soak cherries for an hour. Pit and stew until tender. Clean fish and cut into desired size. Melt butter and in it cook finely chopped vegetables over low heat. Add spices, cherries and seasoning. Combine water and dark beer. Pour over mixture. Place fish in this and simmer until done. Grate gingerbread and peel; chop almonds and raisins and add. Add sugar to taste. Bring to a boil and serve immediately. Serve with Potato Dumplings (No. 195) and Sauerkraut (No. 238).
Serves 4.

90. Carp with Horseradish
(Schleie mit Sahnemeerrettich)

2-3 lbs. carp
1 tbls. vinegar and water
2½ qts. water
1 cup vinegar
salt

For best results carp should be fresh-caught and cleaned under water. Place fish on a moistened platter. Mix the table-spoon of vinegar and water (half and half) and heat. Sprinkle over fish and let stand for 5 minutes. Mix water, vinegar and salt and cook carp in mixture over low heat, for 10 to 15 minutes. Serve on hot platter, with potatoes and Creamed Horseradish, made as follows:

Creamed Horseradish:
½ cup horseradish
1 cup sweet cream
½ tsp. vinegar
pinch of salt
pinch of sugar

Grate horseradish and mix, cold, with slightly beaten sweet cream, vinegar, salt and sugar.

Serves 4.

91. Baked Fillet of Golden Perch
(Goldbarschfilet, gebacken)

2 to 3 lbs. perch
salt
juice of 1 lemon
1 beaten egg or
    ½ cup milk
bread crumbs

Sprinkle fillets of perch with salt and lemon juice. Let stand a short time. Dip into egg or milk, roll in bread crumbs and fry in deep fat until golden brown. The same procedure may be followed with pike or sole. Serve with Potato Salad (No. 258) and Remoulade Sauce (No. 279).

Serves 4.

92.　Codfish or Haddock, Grilled
(Kabeljau oder Schellfisch vom Grill)

2¼ lbs. fish
salt and pepper
juice of 1 lemon
1 tsp. paprika
1 tbls. butter
1 egg
1 tbls. cornstarch
6 tbls. grated cheese

Clean fish and cut in thick slices. Season well with salt and pepper. Sprinkle with lemon juice and let stand. Cream butter, add remaining ingredients and mix well. Coat fish with this and grill for 25 minutes. Serve with Salted Potatoes (No. 199) and a green salad.
Serves 4.

93.　Baked Flounder or Sole
(Flundern oder Schollen, gebacken)

2½ lbs. flounder or sole
salt
lemon juice
milk
bread crumbs
fat
parsley
lemon slices

Clean fish and score lengthwise with sharp knife. Cut off fins and nose. Salt lightly, sprinkle with lemon juice and let stand. Dip in milk, roll in bread crumbs. Fry either in deep fat or in lightly buttered skillet. Garnish with parsley and lemon slices. Serve hot or cold.
Serves 4.

94. Hungarian Codfish *(Kabeljau, ungarische Art)*

1 large onion
2 tbls. butter
2½ lbs. codfish
salt
lemon juice
1 tsp. paprika
1 cup sour cream
1 tsp. cornstarch
½ cup beef stock
extra seasoning

Chop onion and brown in melted butter. Cut fish in portions. Sprinkle with lemon juice, salt and paprika and add to onions. Fry briefly on each side. Pour in cream and cook over low heat for 10 minutes, basting frequently and moving pan gently to prevent sticking. Be careful not to overcook, as this fish tends to break apart. Place on hot platter. Dissolve cornstarch in beef stock and add to drippings. Season well and bring to a boil. Pour over fish to serve. Serve with Salted Potatoes (No. 199), buttered rice or macaroni. Serves 4.

95. Sole *(Scholle, gekocht)*

2½ lbs. sole
2 qts. water
2 tbls. salt
1 tbls. vinegar or
    1 tbls. white wine
parsley
lemon slices

Clean fish and clip fins. Mix all ingredients and cook fish therein for 10 minutes over moderate heat. Remove all of fin which will come out easily when fish is done. Place light side up on hot platter and serve garnished with parsley and lemon slices. Serve with Salted Potatoes (No. 199) and Mustard or Caper Sauce (No. 282). Serves 4.

96. Blue Herring *(Heringe, blau)*

8 herring
¼ cup vinegar, hot
2 qts. water
1 tsp. salt
lemon slices

Clean herring and scald with hot vinegar. Bring salt water to a boil and immerse herring. Lower heat and let simmer for 10 minutes. Place carefully on hot platter and serve garnished with lemon slices. Serve with Salted Potatoes (No. 199) and Creamed Horseradish (No. 90). Serves 4.

97. Grilled Herring *(Heringe vom Rost)*

8-10 herring
salt
8 tbls. flour
olive oil

Remove heads and clean herring. Score backs lightly with a sharp knife. Salt lightly, roll in flour and sprinkle with oil. Put in an oiled or greased pan and cook in a moderate (350°) oven 10 to 15 minutes, or until lightly brown. Serves 4.

98. Herring in Wax Paper *(Heringe in Pergament)*

4 fillets of salt herring
4 fillets of fresh herring
1 onion
1 tbls. fat
wax paper

Skin fillets of salt herring and soak 10 minutes in fresh water. Chop onion and sprinkle over this. Then cover with fillets of fresh herring. Cut wax paper to suitable size. Grease it well and in it roll a pair of herring (both types, with onion sandwiched between). Put 5 inches from medium heat of broiler until paper turns light brown. Or packages may be fried over slow heat in buttered skillet on both sides, until brown. Serves 4.

99. Jellied Herring *(Geleeheringe)*

6 fresh herring
2 cups water
1 tsp. salt
1 onion, chopped
1 cup vinegar
assorted spices
 (peppercorns, etc.)
1 bay leaf
2 envelopes gelatine,
 dissolved in ¼ cup water
½ cup white wine

Clean and cut herring in strips. Combine other ingredients (*except* gelatine and wine) and cook together for 15 minutes. Add herring and simmer for 5 minutes. Remove fish and put in a deep bowl. Dissolve gelatine in water and add to liquid. Season to taste with vinegar (extra) and wine. Pour through strainer over fish. Cool thoroughly and turn out on a platter to serve.
Serves 4-6.

100. Cod in Cream *(Stockfisch)*

2 cups milk
2 cups water
salt
2-2½ lbs. codfish
parsley

Mix milk and water, and while cold, add salt and codfish. Bring to a boil, then lower heat and let simmer for 30 minutes. Drain, remove bones and sprinkle with parsley to serve. Serve with Salted Potatoes (No. 199) and Mustard Sauce (No. 282) or Onion Sauce (No. 283).
Serves 4.

101. Creamed Fish *(Fisch à la Crème)*

2 cups cold cooked fish
 (boned)
1 cup Butter Sauce
 (No. 268)
1 bay leaf, chopped
parsley
½ onion
salt and pepper
¼ cup bread crumbs

Prepare sauce and add bay leaf, parsley and onion. Cook briefly together. Butter oven-proof dish and put in it alternate layers of fish seasoned with salt and pepper and sauce. Cover with bread crumbs and bake in a hot oven (400°) until bread crumbs are well browned.
Serves 2.

102. Fish Rolls (*Fischrouladen*)

2 lbs. fillet of fish
lemon juice
salt
1 onion
2 strips bacon
1 cup pickles
2 tbls. parsley, chopped
flour or bread crumbs
6 tbls. butter

Sprinkle fillets of fish with lemon juice and salt and let stand. Chop onion finely and brown with bacon. Chop pickles and parsley together, and add. Coat fillets with this mixture, roll them up and fasten with toothpicks. Roll in flour or bread crumbs and brown in hot butter. Serve with Salted Potatoes (No. 199) and Tomato Sauce (No. 284) or Sauerkraut Salad (No. 256).

Serves 4.

103. Lobster (*Hummer*)

1 lobster
salt and other seasoning:
vinegar
onions
peppercorns
parsley

Lobster may be bought already cooked and is then red. If bought alive, clean in cold water with a brush. Half fill a large pot with water. Add salt and other desired seasoning such as vinegar, onions, peppercorns, and parsley. Bring to a boil and plunge lobster in head-first. Boil 20 to 30 minutes depending on size of lobster. When done, carve with shears lengthwise through the center of the body and tail, and crack claws. Leave meat in shell, and arrange attractively on a platter. Serve lukewarm or cold. Serve with mayonnaise and bread or, if desired, a vegetable salad garnished with mayonnaise.

Serves 2.

104. Fried Lobster (*Gebratener Hummer*)

1 2-lb. lobster, cooked
   (No. 103)
salt and pepper
lemon juice
bread crumbs
2 egg yolks, beaten
fat

Remove lobster meat, cutting tail section in quarters and leaving claws whole. Season and sprinkle with lemon juice. Dip in bread crumbs, egg yolks, and bread crumbs again. Fry in deep fat. Drain on absorbent paper and serve.
Serves 2.

105. Fried Oysters in Dough (*Gebratene Austern in Teig*)

Dough Beignette (No. 363)
2 doz. oysters
fat
1 lemon, quartered
parsley

Prepare dough. Shuck oysters, wash and dry with towel. Dip in dough and fry in deep fat until brown and crisp. Drain on absorbent paper. Garnish with lemon sections and parsley and serve.
Serves 2-4.

POULTRY *(Geflügel)*

CHICKEN *(Huhn)*

106. Crisp Cockerel *(Gebratener Hahn)*

4-5 lb. roasting chicken
salt
lemon juice
parsley
salt and pepper
3 tbls. butter
1 small onion
¼ cup water

Clean bird and rub inside and out with salt and lemon juice. Dip a small bouquet of parsley in salt and pepper, add to 1 tablespoon butter the heart and liver, cooked and chopped, and stuff into bird. Melt remaining butter, add onion in halves, and lightly brown the bird on all sides. Add water and slowly steam over slow heat, basting from time to time, until tender. Or, after the first light browning and basting, bake until crisp in moderate (350°) oven for 1¼ to 1½ hours. Serve with Fried Potatoes (No. 200), salad and stewed fruit.
Serves 4.

107. Fried Chicken *(Backhähnchen)*

2 fryers
salt and pepper
1 egg
¼ cup bread crumbs
fat or butter
1 lemon, sliced

Have butcher cut chicken in quarters. Clean and rub with salt and pepper. Beat egg and mix with bread crumbs. Roll chicken pieces in this and fry in deep fat. Garnish with lemon slices.
Serves 4-6.

108. Chicken Fricassee (*Hühnerfrikassee*)

1 5-lb. stewing chicken
salt
lemon juice
salted water
4 tbls. butter
1 cup beef stock
2 tbls. flour
1 cup mushrooms
salt and pepper
1 tsp. lemon juice
4 tbls. white wine
1-2 egg yolks
3 tbls. cream

Clean chicken and rub with salt and lemon juice. Boil for five minutes in salted water. Remove and dry with towel. Melt 2 tablespoons of the butter and fry chicken very lightly. Add beef stock, cover and steam until tender, 1½ to 2 hours. Add water, if needed. Remove, carve, skin if desired and keep warm. Melt remaining butter, add flour and blend, add stock and stir until thickened. Add finely chopped mushrooms, seasoning, lemon juice and wine. Thicken with egg yolks and cream. Put chicken slices in this sauce and cook briefly over low flame. Serve with noodles, or rice, and asparagus.
Serves 4-6.

109. Chicken on Rice with Asparagus (*Huhn auf Reis mit Spargel*)

1 5-lb. stewing chicken
Butter Sauce (No. 268)
white wine
salt and pepper
nutmeg
½ tbls. lemon juice
1 to 2 egg yolks
2 lbs. asparagus
1¼ cups rice

Stew chicken until tender, 1½ to 2 hours, skin if desired and cut in slices. Prepare light sauce, using chicken stock in place of water. Add wine to taste, seasonings and lemon juice. Heat chicken in sauce, adding egg yolks to thicken just before serving. Prepare rice and asparagus. Arrange rice on a platter, with chicken on top and asparagus (in piles of 4 to 6 pieces) around this. Pour sauce over it to serve.
Serves 4.

110. Chicken African (*Huhn—afrikanische Art*)

6 shallots
2 garlic cloves
6 cloves
1 small piece of ginger root
1 tbls. paprika
½ tsp. salt and pepper
2 bay leaves
1 3-lb. broiler-fryer
4 tbls. butter

Mash seasonings to a paste. Cut up chicken and spread with paste. Melt butter and brown chicken lightly. Cover and let simmer for 10 minutes. Add hot water to cover and cook until meat is well done, about 20 minutes, and sauce nearly evaporated. Serve with rice.
Serves 3-4.

111. Fried Chicken Livers (*Gebratene Hühnerleber*)

1 slice bacon
2 tbls. butter
1 onion, chopped
6 chicken livers
2 tbls. flour
1 cup Brown Sauce (No. 270)
1 tsp. lemon juice
¼ cup mushrooms, sliced
parsley

Chop up bacon and fry for 5 minutes in butter. Scoop out bacon and save. Add onion and fry for 2 minutes more. Add chicken livers and fry, over moderate heat, for another 2 minutes. Blend in flour, sauce, lemon juice and mushrooms, and cook all together for a final 2 minutes. Crumble up bacon and sprinkle this and parsley over livers. Serve on a hot platter. Very good with Mashed Potatoes (No. 204) or rice.
Serves 3-4.

112. Chicken Soufflé (*Hühner-Soufflé*)

3 tbls. butter
3 tbls. flour
2 cups milk
salt and pepper
¼ cup bread crumbs
2 cups cold, diced chicken
3 eggs, separated
1 tbls. parsley, chopped

Prepare white sauce from the butter, flour, milk and seasoning. Add bread crumbs and cook 2 minutes. Remove from heat and add chicken, egg yolks and chopped parsley. Beat egg whites stiffly and carefully fold in. Butter ovenproof dish, pour in mixture, and bake in moderate heat (350°) for 35 minutes. Veal may be substituted for chicken.
Serves 4.

113. Chicken in Burgundy *(Huhn in Burgunder)*

1 3-lb. broiler-fryer
2 strips of bacon
5 small onions
5 tbls. butter
½ tbls. flour
2 cups Burgundy
1 jigger cognac
1 bay leaf
1 piece of parsley
1 small stalk of thyme
salt, pepper, nutmeg
½ cup button mushrooms,
    chopped

Cut up chicken. Chop up bacon, place in a casserole with onions and butter, and heat thoroughly. Remove and save onions and bacon. Put chicken meat in the casserole, sprinkle with flour and fry, turning frequently, until golden brown. Add Burgundy, cognac and seasonings. Cover and bake in moderate (350°) oven for another 30 minutes. Remove meat and keep warm. Strain sauce through fine sieve. Add onions and bacon, mushrooms, additional butter. Reheat and pour hot over the chicken pieces.
Serves 4.

114. Chicken à La Bonne Femme
(Brathuhn à la bonne Femme)

1 broiler-fryer
salt and pepper
4 tbls. butter
1 onion, chopped
20 small potatoes or slices
1 tbls. paprika
1 cup beef stock
1 cup peas
2 tbls. parsley, chopped
1-2 tbls. white wine

Divide chicken into quarters and rub with salt and pepper. Melt butter, add onion and chicken and brown lightly on all sides. Add potatoes, paprika and beef stock and stew until nearly tender, 15 to 20 minutes. Add peas and parsley and finish cooking, 10 to 15 minutes. Flavor with white wine to taste. To serve, arrange attractively on a warm platter.
Serves 4.

115. Chicken Paprika *(Paprika Huhn)*

1 broiler-fryer
salt and pepper
3-4 tbls. butter
1 medium onion, chopped
1 tbls. paprika
2-3 tbls. flour
¼ cup chicken or beef stock
¼ cup cream

Dress the chicken, divide in quarters and rub with salt and pepper. Brown on all sides in hot butter with onion. Remove chicken, sprinkle paprika in fat, and heat briefly. Add flour and stock. Put back chicken and gently steam it in the sauce, in a well-covered pan, for about 20 minutes. Pour in cream, heat. Add salt and paprika to taste.

Serves 4.

116. Capon *(Poularde)*

1 6-lb. capon
salt and pepper
lemon juice
large slice of bacon
1 cup water
1 onion
4 tbls. butter

Stuffing:
2 rolls
2 eggs
liver and heart
salt, pepper and nutmeg

Rub inside and out with salt, pepper and lemon juice. Prepare stuffing, if desired, by crumbling rolls, adding beaten eggs, chopped liver and heart, and seasonings. Stuff and sew up the bird. (If not to be stuffed, put in parsley, butter and one chopped truffle.) Cover breast with bacon and place in casserole. Add water and sliced onion, season, cover, and roast in 350° oven until tender, about 2 hours. When the water has evaporated, the bird should be crisply browned on all sides in its own fat. Cooking time, slightly over one hour unstuffed, an hour and a half stuffed.

Variation: Steam bird in 1 cup water in a covered pot for 1½ hours (adding more water if necessary). Pour melted butter over, place in 450° oven and roast until brown, 20 to 30 minutes, basting frequently. Remove when done and add flour and water to make gravy. Serve with green salad or spring vegetables and new potatoes.

Serves 4-6.

GOOSE *(Gans)*

117.   Stuffed Goose *(Gefüllte Gans)*

1 goose, medium size
salt and pepper
lemon juice
1 tbls. flour
2 cups water

Clean goose thoroughly. Rub with salt, pepper and lemon juice inside and out. Let stand for 2 hours. Stuff as desired (see below), sew up incision and truss. Place in a roaster, pour on hot water, cover and let it steam until it begins to fry in its own fat. The underside near the drumstick may be pierced to release additional fat. Turn goose now and then to obtain an even brown all around. Uncover and roast in 325° oven for 1 to 2 hours, depending on age of the bird. Continue to turn and baste frequently. If a deeper, crisper brown is desired, brush with melted butter. Add flour and water to the fat and season well for gravy. Skim off any surface fat before serving. Serve with Potato Dumplings (No. 195) or Salted Potatoes (No. 199) and Red Cabbage (No. 227), followed by stewed fruits or berries.

Stuffings:
(a)
3 rolls
1 cup milk
1 onion, chopped
1 tsp. parsley, chopped
1 tbls. butter
heart and liver, cooked
2 eggs, separated
salt, pepper and nutmeg

Stuffings:
(a) Soak rolls in milk. Press dry and pluck to pieces. Sauté onion and parsley in butter. Add rolls and remove from heat. Chop heart and liver, and blend with egg yolks. Fold in beaten egg whites. Blend well with first mixture and season to taste.

(b)
1 onion, chopped
1 tsp. parsley, chopped
1 tbls. butter
heart and liver, cooked
½ cup potatoes, boiled
1 egg, beaten
cream
salt and pepper

(b) Sauté onion and parsley in butter. Add chopped heart and liver. Dice potatoes and add, together with lightly beaten egg and cream. Season to taste.

(c)
1½ lbs. chestnuts
1 tsp. sugar
1 tbls. butter
1 cup beef stock
salt

(c) Incise chestnuts crosswise. Roast in oven and remove shells. Brown sugar lightly in butter. Add chestnuts and beef stock. Season with salt and boil 20 minutes.

118. Goose Liver Cutlet (*Gänseleberschnitzel*)

1 goose liver
paprika
3 tbls. flour
1 tbls. butter
½ cup port wine
1 truffle
salt and pepper
2 cups seedless grapes

Slice liver ½ inch thick. Sprinkle with paprika and dip lightly in flour. Brown in butter, remove and keep warm. Add to the drippings, the wine and sliced truffle. Thicken sauce with more flour. Season and add some of the seedless grapes. Pour sauce over liver. Garnish with remaining grapes. Serve with Mashed Potatoes (No. 204).
Serves 2.

119. Goose Liver with Apples (*Gänseleber mit Äpfeln*)

1 goose liver
1 tbls. flour
1 tbls. butter
1 apple
1 onion
salt and pepper

Slice liver and dip in flour. Brown in butter on both sides. Remove cover, and let stand on a hot platter in a warm place. Chop up apple and onion and fry in fat. Add to liver and season to taste. Add a little water to the fat, heat and pour over liver dish. Serve with Mashed Potatoes (No. 204).
Serves 2.

DUCKLING *(Ente)*

120. Roast Duckling *(Gebratene Ente)*

1 5-lb. duckling
salt and pepper
2 tbls. butter
1 onion, chopped
flour
2 cups beef stock

Clean duck and rub inside and out with salt and pepper. Stuff, if desired. Chop onion and add to melted butter in Dutch oven or casserole and brown duck in this on all sides. Add meat stock or water, cover and cook until done. After liquid has evaporated, turn over now and then, adding water by spoonfuls, until duck is well done and crisp.

Alternate method: Cook on top of range until *nearly* done. Remove, pour on butter and roast uncovered in 450° oven until well done. Cooking time about one hour; if stuffed, an hour and a quarter. Remove from oven.

Prepare gravy from drippings, flour and beef stock. Serve with Red Cabbage (No. 227) and Salted Potatoes (No. 199).

Stuffings:
(a)
2 small rolls
1 small onion
parsley
1 tbls. butter
liver and heart, cooked
1-2 eggs
salt and pepper
nutmeg

(b)
½ cup bread crumbs
½ cup chopped nuts
½ cup sweet cream
2 tbls. butter
dash onion juice
salt and pepper

Stuffings:
(a) Soak rolls in water. Sauté finely chopped onion and parsley in butter. Add the rolls, squeezed dry, and simmer together. Chop liver and heart; add, with eggs and seasoning, to mixture.

(b) Mix all ingredients in order given.

TURKEY *(Truthahn)*

121. Roast Turkey *(Truthahn vom Rost)*

1 12-lb. turkey
salt
1 cup butter
¼ cup flour
½ cup butter melted in
    ½ cup water

Prepare stuffing (No. 122). Stuff turkey and sew up. Rub entire turkey with salt. Cream butter, mix in flour and spread on breast, legs and wings. Sprinkle flour in roasting pan, place bird on its back. Put in a hot (500°) oven. When the flour on the turkey begins to brown, reduce heat to 300°. Baste every 15 minutes with butter melted in water. Cook 20 minutes to the pound, turning the bird frequently to ensure even browning. If any part gets too dark, butter wax paper and place on that part. Garnish with parsley, celery tips and crisp leaves and with rings cut from sliced yellow turnips. Serve with Mashed Potatoes (No. 204) and Wine-Cabbage or mixed vegetables or a salad plate.

Wine Cabbage:
Sauerkraut (No. 238)
2 cups sauterne

Wine-Cabbage is steamed sauerkraut to which 2 cups of sauterne have been added and allowed almost to evaporate.
    Serves 8.

122. Turkey Stuffing *(Truthahnfülle)*

1½ 1-lb. loaves of bread
⅓ cup salted pork fat
heart and liver
1 egg
salt and pepper
sage or truffle

Toast bread a light brown, cut off crusts and moisten with water. Chop up fat, the turkey heart and liver and put, with toast, through meat grinder. Add beaten egg, seasoning to taste and mix well with sage or truffle.

123. Turkey Croquettes (*Truthahnkroketten*)

1 cup chopped cooked
   turkey
⅔ cup chopped cooked ham
6 mushrooms
2 tbls. butter
1 cup beef stock
2 tbls. butter
salt and pepper
parsley
2 eggs, separated
bread crumbs
fat

Chop turkey and ham finely and mix. Chop mushrooms and sauté in butter and add. Cook beef stock until half has evaporated. Add butter, seasoning and chopped parsley and cook for 10 minutes over slow heat. Put through strainer and thicken with egg yolks. Blend meat mixture with this sauce and let cool. Shape into croquettes. Beat egg whites stiffly and dip croquettes twice, alternately, in egg white and bread crumbs. Fry in deep fat. Serve with any kind of salad.
Serves 3-4.

GAME (*Wildbret*)

124. Pheasant (*Fasan*)

1 pheasant
salt and pepper
large slice bacon
butter
½ cup cream
1 tbls. flour
1 cup beef stock

Rub pheasant inside and out with salt and pepper and cover breast with bacon. Melt butter in casserole and roast pheasant in it, basting frequently, in a medium (350°) oven for about an hour. Pour cream over it and return briefly to the oven. Remove from casserole and keep warm. To the drippings add flour and blend smoothly. Add beef stock and stir until gravy thickens slightly. Serve with Mashed Potatoes (No. 204) and Champagne-Cabbage, same as Wine-Cabbage (No. 121) but with champagne.
Serves 4.

125.   Partridge—Grouse *(Rebhuhn, Haselhuhn)*

4 young partridges or
   grouse
salt and pepper
3 tbls. butter
¼ cup juniper berries,
   optional
4 strips bacon
3 tbls. butter
1 small onion
1 cup cream, heated

Clean and rub birds inside and out with salt and pepper. Mix butter and juniper berries and put one-fourth portion into each bird. Encircle with bacon, put in casserole. Melt butter and pour over. Add onion and seasoning, to taste. Bake in hot (400°) oven for about 20 minutes, basting frequently. Pour on cream and serve. Serve with Mashed Potatoes (No. 204) and Wine-Cabbage (No. 121).
Serves 4.

126.   False Partridge *(Falsche Rebhühner)*

2 large, fat squabs
1 cup water
5 tbls. vinegar
1 bay leaf
1 clove
1 onion
peppercorns
salt and pepper
¼ cup juniper berries
salt and pepper
2 strips bacon
2 tbls. butter
1 onion
¼ cup beef stock
1 tsp. flour
¼ cup cream

Dress squabs. Combine water, vinegar, bay leaf, clove, onion, peppercorns, salt and pepper, and cook for 5 minutes. Let squabs soak overnight in this steeping liquid. Remove birds, dry and sprinkle with seasoning and crushed juniper berries. Wrap bacon around. Brown in hot butter, add chopped onion and beef stock. Cover and simmer about 40 minutes, or roast in 400° oven about 45 minutes, turning and basting occasionally. Remove birds, thicken fat with flour and add cream to make sauce.
Serves 2.

MEAT (*Fleisch*)

VEAL (*Kalbfleisch*)

127. Veal Cutlet (*Schnitzel, naturell*)

¾ lb. veal cutlet, ½" thick
1 tsp. olive oil
salt and pepper
2 tbls. butter
paprika
1 lemon, quartered

Soak cutlet in milk for 10 minutes. Dry, pound lightly, brush with oil and seasoning. Fry slowly in hot butter, on both sides, for about 25 minutes. When done, sprinkle with paprika. Garnish with quartered lemon. Serve with rice, potatoes or dumplings; with cauliflower, spinach or green salad.
Serves 2.

128. Paprika Cutlet with Cream (*Paprika-Rahmschnitzel*)

¾ lb. veal cutlet, 1½" thick
salt
2 tbls. butter
paprika
¼ tsp. flour
2-3 tbls. cream
lemon, sliced
parsley

Pound cutlet and season with salt. Fry slowly on both sides in butter for 25 minutes. Sprinkle generously with paprika, turn over once in fat and put on a warm platter. To the fat add flour and cream. Cook together briefly and pour this sauce over cutlet. Garnish with lemon slices, topped alternately with paprika and chopped parsley. Serve with rolls or dumplings, or buttered rice and a salad.
Serves 2.

129. Wiener Schnitzel

½ lb. veal cutlet, ¼" thick
salt and pepper
1 egg
¼ cup bread crumbs
fat
lemon
parsley

Pound cutlet, rub in seasoning. Beat egg and dip cutlet in egg and in bread crumbs. Brown in minimum amount of melted fat over low heat, 15 minutes on each side. Schnitzel must be served dry and crisp. Garnish with lemon sections and parsley. Bundles of parsley may be fried in fat until crisp to garnish. Serve on hot platter. Serve with mixed vegetables, peas, or a mixed salad.

Serves 2.

130. Veal Birds *(Kalbfleischvögel)*

1 onion
parsley
3 tbls. butter
3 anchovies or
    anchovy paste
1 lb. veal (leg)
½ cup water
1 tbls. flour
½ cup or more cream
salt, pepper, lemon juice to
    taste

Chop onion and parsley finely and stew in 1 tablespoon of butter. Wash anchovies and mix in. Have veal sliced very thin, pound and spread with spicy mixture. Roll up and fasten with toothpicks. Melt remaining butter in skillet and brown rolls lightly. Add water and stew until done, about 30 minutes. When water has evaporated, remove birds, add flour and enough cream to make desired amount of gravy. Season to taste. Serve with Mashed Potatoes (No. 204).

Serves 3-4.

131. Loin of Veal Trianon *(Kalbsnuss Trianon)*

1 lb. loin of veal
2 ozs. tongue
a few truffles
2 strips of bacon
3 tbls. butter
1 cup beef stock
1 tbl. flour
2 tbls. cream
seasoning to taste

Remove skin and lard loin with slivers of tongue, truffles and bacon. Sprinkle lightly with salt. Brown in butter on all sides. Add beef stock and stew until tender, about 1 hour. When stock has evaporated, brown flour in pan and add water to make desired amount of gravy. Add cream and season to taste. Serve with Cauliflower, Polish Style (No. 219). Serves 3-4.

132. Veal Chops, Plain *(Kalbskoteletten, naturell)*

2 veal chops
salt and pepper
2 tbls. flour
3 tbls. butter
lemon, sliced

Pound and rub chops with seasoning. Dip in flour and brown lightly in hot butter on both sides. Reduce heat and let simmer until done through, about 25 minutes. Garnish with lemon to serve. Serve with lima beans, spinach, cauliflower or other vegetables. Serves 2.

133. Calf's Liver *(Kalbsleber)*

1 lb. calf's liver, sliced
milk
flour
2 tbls. butter
1 onion, sliced in rings
1 tsp. flour
½ cup water
salt and pepper

Dip liver in milk, then flour; fry, with onion rings, in butter. Place on hot platter and heap crisp onion rings on top. Add flour to pan and brown. Add water and seasoning to taste and bring to a boil. Strain gravy and serve in separate gravy boat to prevent onions from losing their crispness. Serve with Mashed Potatoes (No. 204) and a salad. Serves 2-3.

134. Calf's Liver with Bacon (Kalbsleber mit Speck)

1 lb. calf's liver, sliced
flour to dip
4 strips bacon
2 tbls. butter
salt and pepper

Dip liver in flour. Fry liver and bacon together in hot butter on both sides. Season and arrange on a hot plate. Serve with rice or potatoes.

Serves 2-3.

135. Liver and Kidney, Sour (Saure Leber und Nieren)

4 lamb kidneys
1 lb. calf's liver
2 tbls. butter
1 onion
1 tbls. flour
½-1 cup water
1 tbls. vinegar
salt and pepper

Slice kidneys thin. Brown with liver in hot butter. Place on a hot plate. Chop onion and add, with flour, to pan. Brown. Add water to desired consistency, and stir until blended. Add vinegar and seasonings. Return meat and bring mixture to a boil. Serve with Salted (No. 199) or Fried Potatoes (No. 200).

Serves 4.

136. Veal Kidneys (Kalbsnieren)

2 veal kidneys
4 tbls. butter
salt and pepper
1 tbls. flour
1 cup water

Slice kidneys and their fat. Fry in butter over strong heat until done, about 8 minutes. Season and serve. Or remove from fat, add flour and water and cook briefly. Season and pour over kidneys. Serve with Mashed Potatoes (No. 204).

Serves 4.

137. Brains in Brown Butter
(Hirn in brauner Butter)

2 calf's brains
4 tbls. butter
1 tbls. capers
lemon juice
salt and pepper

Soak brains in cold water for 1 hour. Drain and remove membrane. Simmer 20 minutes in salted water with 1 tablespoon vinegar added. Drain thoroughly and chop coarsely. Brown butter lightly and add brains. Stir while cooking. Add capers, a dash of lemon juice and salt and pepper to taste. These can be further seasoned with ketchup or a sharp salad dressing. Serve with Salted Potatoes (No. 199).

Serves 4.

138. Baked Brains (Gebackener Hirn)

2 calf's brains
salt and pepper
1 egg
bread crumbs
fat
lemon slices
parsley

Soak brains in cold water 1 hour, remove membrane, and cook for 5 minutes in salted water. Remove and cool. Cut each in three parts. Sprinkle well with seasoning. Tumble in beaten egg and in bread crumbs. Brown in hot fat. Garnish with lemon slices and parsley. Serve with Potato Salad (No. 258) and Remoulade Sauce (No. 279).

Serves 4.

139. Veal Roast (*Kalbsbraten*)

5-6 lbs. leg or shoulder
of veal
salt and pepper
4 tbls. butter
1 onion
1 tomato
1 cup beef stock
butter
1 tbls. flour
paprika

Sprinkle meat with salt and pepper and brown on all sides in hot butter. Chop onion and tomato and add to meat. Add beef stock, cover and cook in slow (300°) oven 1¼ hours, adding more liquid if needed. When meat is done, liquid should be evaporated. Add butter and fry meat until it looks glazed and crisp. Serve sliced, on a hot platter. To drippings, add flour, paprika and as much water as needed for desired amount of gravy. Strain well and serve in gravy boat. Serve with dumplings, Spätzle (No. 196) or potatoes and vegetables or salad. Serves 4.

140. Stuffed Breast of Veal (*Gefüllte Kalbsbrust*)

5-6 lbs. breast of veal
salt
lemon juice
4 rolls
1 cup milk
1 onion
1 or 2 eggs
parsley
salt and pepper
1 cup (or more) beef stock
1 onion
1 tbls. flour
salt, pepper, nutmeg

Have butcher make a pocket in the meat. Rub insides with salt and lemon juice. Make stuffing as follows:

Cut up rolls and simmer briefly in milk. Cool. Chop onion and cook without browning in a little fat. Add to bread mixture. Beat egg and add, with parsley and seasoning. Mix well and stuff into pocket. Sew up.

Heat beef stock. Chop second onion and add. Cook veal in stock, covered, 1¼ hours. Turn now and then and add liquid if necessary. Or roast in moderate (350°) oven for 1½ hours. Remove from pan, add flour and seasoning and as much liquid as desired for gravy. Slice meat with a very sharp knife to prevent stuffing from crumbling. Serve with Spätzle (No. 196) and a green salad. Serves 6.

141. Veal Shank (*Kalbshaxe*)

1 bunch carrots
2 onions
2 pieces celery
salt and pepper
1 large (3-4 lbs.) veal shank
3 tbls. butter
1 tbls. vinegar
1 tbls. flour
water, or stock

Cook vegetables and seasoning in a large pot in just enough water to cover them. When cooked, add shank of veal and cook 2 to 3 hours over very low heat, adding more water when necessary. Remove shank and brown in hot butter until crisp. The vegetable water provides a fine base for soup.

Variation: Season shank and fry briefly with chopped onion in butter, turning now and then. Add water as desired, cover and cook over low heat for 2 to 3 hours. Remove. Add vinegar, flour, water or stock to make gravy. Pour gravy over shank to serve. Serve with Potato Salad (No. 258), green salad or mixed vegetables.
Serves 4.

142. Veal Roast, Polish (*Polnischer Kalbsbraten*)

4-5 lb. boned veal roast
lemon juice
salt and pepper
1 slice bacon
1 tbls. pickle
3 anchovies
6 tbls. butter
¼ cup sour cream

Rub meat with lemon juice, salt and pepper. Lard with slivers of bacon, pickle and anchovies. Follow method of No. 139. Prepare gravy with butter and sour cream, add seasoning to taste. Serve with Mashed Potatoes (No. 204) or dumplings or Spätzle (No. 196) and a green salad.
Serves 4-6.

143. Genuine Hungarian Pickled Veal (*Echter ungarischer Pörkelt*)

2-lb. shoulder of boned veal
2 large onions
4 tbls. bacon grease
1 cup beef stock
salt and pepper
paprika
1 tsp. caraway seeds

Have meat cut in large chunks. Chop onions finely and fry with meat in very hot bacon grease. Add beef stock and seasoning, cover and simmer until onions have disappeared, about 1½ hours. Serve with Salted Potatoes (No. 199) or dumplings and Sauerkraut (No. 238). Serves 4-5.

144. Veal Goulash (*Kalbsgulasch*)

3-lb. breast of boned veal
2 onions
3 tbls. butter
1-2 tomatoes
1 cup water
salt and pepper
paprika
3 tbls. flour
extra water

Have meat cut in large cubes. Chop onions finely and brown with meat in butter. Peel and slice tomatoes. Combine with onion and meat, add water and seasoning. Cover and stew until done, about 1½ hours. Just before it is done, remove cover and let water evaporate. Sprinkle in flour and brown. Add water enough to make suitable amount of gravy. Serve with potatoes or dumplings, and a salad. Serves 4.

145. Pickled Veal (*Eingemachtes Kalbfleisch*)

3-lb. breast of veal
2-3 tbls. butter
1 small onion, chopped
salt and pepper
peppercorns
1 bay leaf
3 tbls. flour
½ cup white wine (sauterne)
dash of lemon juice
1 egg yolk
1 tbls. diced mushrooms,
    optional

Have meat cut into palm-size slices. Scald by placing briefly in boiling water. Melt butter. Cook, but do not brown, meat and onion in the butter. Add water to cover; add seasonings and cook about 1½ hours. Dissolve flour in a little water, add to stew together with wine and lemon juice, to taste. Cook briefly and thicken with egg yolk. A few mushrooms may be added. Serve with noodles or buttered rice. Serves 4.

146. Calf's Head *(Kalbskopf, gekocht)*

¼ calf's head
soup greens
salt and pepper
pickling spices
1 bay leaf
1 onion

Clean calf's head and cook in water to cover with soup greens and seasonings 1 hour or until tender. Cut into suitable portions and serve.

Serves 4.

147. Loin of Veal, Cold *(Kalte Kalbslende)*

2 lbs. loin of veal boned
    and rolled
bacon to lard
2 onions
carrots, diced
1 soup bone
¼ lb. soup greens
salt and pepper
½ cup red wine
2 tsp. cognac
1 cucumber
1-2 tbls. butter

Lard a rolled loin roast with bacon and tie with string. Cook together the onions, carrots, soup bone, greens and seasoning for 20 minutes in a deep pot. Add wine, cognac and the meat and cook, over moderate heat, for 2 hours, turning meat over from time to time. Add water or beef stock as needed. When meat is done, remove string and place meat in a tureen. Slice cucumber ½ inch thick and sauté in butter until tender. Garnish meat with cucumber. Stir gravy and cook until very smooth, ladling off excess fat, then strain over meat. Chill and serve cold.

Serves 5-6.

BEEF (*Rindfleisch*)

148. Rumpsteak Entrecote (*Rumpsteak, Entrecôte*)

1 lb. rump steak
bacon slivers
1 tbls. oil
3 tbls. butter
salt and pepper
½ cup beef stock

Choose a particularly tender, properly aged piece of meat. Lard it with bacon. Rub all over with oil and crisp on all sides in a very hot pan, using no added fat. Add butter, salt, pepper and beef stock. Cover and let simmer for 5-10 minutes over low heat, depending upon how rare you want it. Serve with Alsatian Fried Potatoes (No. 206) and Sauce Bernaise (No. 273) or finely mixed vegetables or salad. Serves 2-3.

149. Filet Mignon (*Lendenschnitten Filetbeefsteak*)

1 lb. filet mignon
1 tbls. oil
salt and pepper
2 tomatoes
2 tbls. butter
Herb Butter (No. 299)
2 fried eggs, optional

Have filet cut in two pieces, each 1½ inches thick. Pound, spread with oil and sprinkle with seasoning. Broil for 6 to 10 minutes (depending on how rare you like it), close to heat, or pan broil on both sides in a very hot skillet until crisp on both sides. Add butter, cover, and let simmer for a few minutes. Wash and dry tomatoes. Slice and fry in butter, or grill in oven. Garnish steaks with tomatoes and dabs of Herb Butter, or top with fried eggs. Serve with Alsatian Fried Potatoes (No. 206), salad or mixed vegetables. Serves 2.

150. Roast Beef (Rostbraten)

3½ lbs. boneless rib roast
1 tbls. oil
1 cup water
½ cup cream
salt and pepper
1 tbls. cornstarch

Rub meat with oil and brown on all sides in a skillet, turning frequently. Put in a casserole, add water and transfer to 375° oven. Cook for 30 to 40 minutes depending on rareness desired. Pour on cream, add seasoning. Turn off heat but let simmer in oven for a few more minutes. Remove roast from pan. To the drippings add cornstarch and water to make gravy. Let roast cool down before carving, so juices run through it. Serve on hot platter, garnished with parsley. Serve with Alsatian Fried Potatoes (No. 206) and spinach or mixed vegetables. Serves 5-6.

151. Sirloin Roast (Lendenbraten)

3-lb. sirloin roast
1 slice bacon, slivered
salt and pepper
1 onion
1 tomato
4 tbls. butter
½ cup water
2 tbls. flour
1 cup sour cream
¼ cup white wine
salt and pepper
paprika

Lard meat with fine slivers of bacon. Season with salt and pepper. Slice onion and tomato. Brown roast, tomato and onion slices in butter over strong heat. Add water and transfer pan to hot oven (400°) and cook, basting frequently, 30 to 40 minutes, depending on desired rareness. Remove meat. To drippings add flour, cream, wine and seasonings. Cook together briefly. Slice roast and pour sauce over servings. Serve with Spätzle (No. 196), or noodles, and salad. Serves 6.

152. Goulash Filet *(Filetgulasch)*

1 onion
3 tbls. butter
¾-lb. filet of beef
salt and pepper
1 tbls. flour
1 cup beef stock
2 tbls. white wine

Chop onion and brown in butter. Cube meat and add. Season. Brown quickly over strong heat. Sprinkle with flour, add beef stock and wine and simmer for 5 minutes more. Serve with Niedernauer Potatoes (No. 201) or Mashed Potatoes (No. 204).
Serves 2.

153. Sauerbraten

½ cup vinegar
½ cup water
1 onion, sliced
salt and pepper
1 bay leaf
1 clove
1½ lbs. beef (shoulder)
1 marrow bone
2 tbls. fat
1 onion
1 tomato

Sauce:
1 tbls. flour
vinegar or lemon juice
pinch of sugar
salt
butter
cream or wine

Cook vinegar, water, sliced onion and seasoning together for 10 minutes. Steep beef in this marinade 2 to 3 days. Drain (save liquid). Brown meat and marrow bone in hot fat. Add the onion, tomato and ½ cup of the marinade, cover and simmer on top of range for 1 hour. Turn the meat in remaining liquid so that it is coated on all sides. Carve and put on a warm platter.
For sauce, mix flour with pan liquid smoothly. Add the rest of the marinade and stir until smooth and thickened. Sauerbraten sauce calls for more ample ingredients than other sauces. Add, to taste, a little vinegar or lemon juice, a pinch of sugar, salt, a little fresh butter and a tablespoon of cream or wine. Strain and pour over meat or serve as a separate sauce. Serve with potatoes, dumplings or Spätzle (No. 196).
Serves 3-4.

154. Pot Roast (*Schmorbraten*)

2-lb. rump roast
salt and pepper
1 marrow bone
2 tbls. butter
1 onion
1 tomato
½ cup water
1 tbls. flour
½ cup beef stock
½ cup cream

Rub roast liberally with salt and pepper and fry, with the marrow bone, in butter over strong heat. Dice onion and tomato and add. Pour in water, cover and stew for 1½ to 2 hours, turning from time to time. Add water as needed. Place roast on hot platter. To fat add flour, beef stock and cream to make gravy. Put through fine strainer and into gravy boat. Serve with Salted Potatoes (No. 199) and Curly Cabbage (No. 225); noodles or Spätzle (No. 196) and salad.
Serves 4.

155. Beef Goulash (*Rindergulasch*)

1 lb. beef chuck, cubed
2-3 onions
2-3 tbls. butter
salt and pepper
paprika
1 cup water
2 tbls. flour
1 cup beef stock
3 tomatoes, sliced

Chop onions and brown in butter. Add meat and seasonings. Fry meat until browned. Add water, cover, and let stew for one hour. When juice has evaporated, sprinkle with flour, brown lightly; add beef stock and sliced tomatoes and cook together briefly. Serve with noodles, Spätzle (No. 196), Salted (No. 199) or Fried Potatoes (No. 200).
Serves 2.

156. Beef Rolls (*Rinderrouladen*)

4 thin slices of beef
salt and pepper
4 slices bacon
1 onion
1 tbls. parsley
1 tbls. mustard
1 tbls. flour
2 tbls. butter
½ cup water
extra flour
2 tbls. cream
salt and pepper
paprika
2 tbls. beef stock

Pound beef slices and rub with salt and pepper. Cut up bacon, chop onion and parsley and mix all with mustard. Spread this on beef slices and roll up tightly. Tie with string. Dip rolls in flour and fry in butter, to brown all sides. Add water and stew for 30 minutes. When water has evaporated, turn rolls once again. Remove, untie and place on hot platter. To "*Bratensatz*" in pan, add flour, cream, seasonings and beef stock to make gravy. Pour over meat. Serve with Salted Potatoes (No. 199) or Mashed Potatoes (No. 204) and a salad.
Serves 4.

157. Ground Beef Patties (*Gehacktes Rinderschnitzel*)

1 cooked potato
1 onion
1 lb. ground beef
1 egg
salt and pepper
⅔ tbls. butter
1 tsp. cornstarch
¼ cup water or stock

Grate potato, chop onion and mix well with ground meat, egg and seasoning. Form into cakes and fry in butter on both sides, for a total of 8 to 10 minutes over medium high heat, basting occasionally. Prepare gravy from fat, cornstarch and water or beef stock. Or use Onion Butter (No. 311). Serve with Salted Potatoes (No. 199) and salad or vegetables.
Serves 2.

158. German Beefsteak *(Deutsches Beefsteak)*

1 onion
¾ lb. chopped beef
1 tbls. flour
2 tbls. water
pinch of pepper
1 tsp. salt
3 tbls. butter
½ onion, sliced
extra flour for gravy

Chop onion and mix well with ground meat, flour, water and seasoning. Form into oblong patties. With finger press a hole in the center of each patty, fill with butter and close over. Fry in butter on both sides, 3 to 5 minutes. Remove. Brown sliced onion in fat and place on patties. Add flour and water to fat, cooking briefly and blending well to form gravy. Pour this over patties and serve with Potato Salad (No. 258) or Mashed Potatoes (No. 204) and a salad. Serves 2.

159. Hamburger Loaf *(Hackbraten)*

2 onions
2 tbls. parsley
3 tbls. butter
3 rolls
1 lb. mixed ground meat
    (½ lb. beef, ½ lb. pork)
1 egg
1 tbls. flour
salt and pepper
bread crumbs
½ cup beef stock

Chop one onion with parsley and brown in butter. Cube rolls and add. Mix well with meat, egg, flour and seasoning. Shape into oblong loaf, roll in bread crumbs and fry on both sides over medium high heat. Add second onion chopped, pour on water as needed, cover and cook over slow heat until done. Shortly before it is done, remove cover, increase heat and fry until crisp. Or bake in oven for about one hour, basting frequently. Remove loaf and prepare gravy from flour and beef stock, stirring and cooking over low heat until smooth; or use Onion Butter (No. 296). Serve with Salted Potatoes (No. 199) vegetables or salad. Serves 4-6.

160.   Onion-Beef *(Zwiebelfleisch)*

4 slices leftover meat
1 onion
1 tbls. butter
salt and pepper
2-4 eggs
    or pancake batter
parsley

Slice beef (or other leftover meat) thinly and season well. Chop onion and brown in butter along with meat, browning meat on both sides. Meat may be topped with fried eggs, or dipped in pancake batter and fried. Serve on a hot platter garnished with parsley. Serve with Potato Salad (No. 258) or Fried Potatoes (No. 200) and a green salad.

Serves 2.

161.   Spiced Kidneys *(Saure Nieren)*

1 beef kidney
1 onion
3 tbls. butter
1 tbls. flour
1 tbls. vinegar
dash of lemon juice
pepper
3 tbls. white wine
¼ cup soup stock
salt

Remove fat from kidney. Chop onion finely and brown in butter. Slice kidney very thin and add. Stew until tender. When done, kidney color will change from pink to gray throughout. Remove and keep on hot platter. To fat, add all remaining ingredients except salt. Cook together 5 minutes, cut off heat; replace kidneys and let soak in sauce 5 minutes. Add salt to taste, at the very end just before serving, as it will otherwise harden kidneys. Serve with Salted Potatoes (No. 199) or Spätzle (No. 196).

Serves 2-4.

162. Ox Tongue in Madeira
(Ochsenzunge in Madeira)

1 salted ox tongue
soup greens
1 onion

Soak tongue in fresh water for an hour. Then cook together with soup greens and chopped onion in unsalted water for 3 to 4 hours. Tongue is done if skin peels off easily. Be sure to remove all skin. Slice tongue and serve with Madeira Sauce (No. 271), Mashed Potatoes (No. 204) and spinach or young green beans. Serves 6-8.

163. Ragout of Tongue (Zungenragout)

1 cup cubed tongue
Caper Sauce (No. 282) or
  Madeira Sauce (No. 271)

This is a good dish for leftover tongue or tongue prepared as in No. 162. Slice or cube meat and cook, until thoroughly heated, in sauce of your choice. Serves 2.

164. Ox-Tail Ragout (Ochsenschweifragout)

1 oxtail
water to cover
½ tsp. salt
2 onions
3 turnips
2 tomatoes
1 stalk celery
2 tbls. butter
½ cup white wine
1 bay leaf
2 cloves
salt and pepper
paprika
flour

Have oxtail cut in pieces the size of links of its bones. Cook 5 minutes in salted water. Dry in a strainer. Dice vegetables. Melt butter and add meat and vegetables, and fry. Add wine, seasonings, some soup stock, if necessary, to cover meat. Cover and cook 2 to 3 hours, until done. Remove meat. Add flour to juice to prepare smooth gravy. Add more wine and further seasoning, to taste. Pour over meat. Serve with Spätzle (No. 196) or Mashed Potatoes (No. 204). Serves 4.

PORK (Schweinfleisch)

165. Pork Chops
(Schweinekoteletten auf drierlei Art)

4 pork chops
salt and pepper
1 egg, beaten
bread crumbs
1 tbls. butter

Here are three methods for cooking pork chops:
1. Rub chops generously on both sides with salt and pepper. Dip in egg and in bread crumbs. Fry slowly in butter until crisp and thoroughly done.
2. Season chops well and fry slowly in butter until crisp.
3. Broil chops slowly on both sides 5 inches from heat. Season well when done. Serve with Potato Salad (No. 258), Cucumber Salad (No. 244) or cooked carrots and mixed vegetables.
Serves 4.

166. Pork Chops, with Mustard or Horseradish
(Schweinekoteletten mit Senf oder Meerrettich)

4 pork chops
salt and pepper
4 tbls. mustard or 4 tbls.
    horseradish with 2 tsp.
    vinegar
2 tbls. butter
1 cup beef stock or 1 cup
    white wine (or both)
2 tbls. sour cream

Season chops well and spread both sides with seasoning and either mustard or a paste of horseradish and vinegar. Let stand for several hours. Melt butter and lightly brown chops on both sides. Add beef stock or wine, or ½ cup of each. Cover and stew, over low heat, until chops are done through, about ½ hour. Serve with Mashed Potatoes (No. 204) and a salad.
Serves 4.

167. Pork Chops with Apples
(Schweinekoteletten mit gebratenen Äpfeln)

2 pork chops
2 tbls. butter
2 apples

Fry unseasoned pork chops in butter. Remove to a hot platter. Slice apples ½ inch thick and fry in same butter. Arrange apples around the chops on the platter. Serves 2.

168. Pork Schnitzel (Schweineschnitzel)

4-8 loin pork chops
salt and pepper
2 tbls. butter
1 onion, sliced

Pound chops lightly and season. Fry in butter, with onion, on both sides, quickly over high heat. Reduce heat, cover and let simmer 20 minutes more. Serve with Salted Potatoes (No. 199) and vegetables. Serves 4.

169. Pork Tenderloin Fillets (Schweinefilet)

1 lb. pork tenderloin
salt and pepper
2 tbls. butter
1 onion, sliced
1 tomato, sliced
1 tbls. flour
¼ cup beef stock
1 tbls. sour cream
¼ cup white wine

Slice pork into fillets ¾ inch thick, pound lightly and season well. Fry in butter, over high heat, on both sides, together with sliced onion and tomato. Reduce heat and simmer 20 to 30 minutes. Add flour to fat to form gravy, thinning with beef stock. Add cream and wine, strain well, and pour over fillets. Serves 4.

170. Pork Rolls *(Schweinerouladen)*

2 lbs. pork (leg meat)
1 onion, chopped
parsley, chopped
1 egg, beaten
salt and pepper
1 roll
1 tbls. prepared mustard or
    pinch of marjoram
5 tbls. flour
2 tbls. butter
1 cup stock or water

Grind a half pound of the meat in meat-grinder. Slice the rest thinly and pound lightly. Mix ground pork with chopped onion, parsley, egg, salt and pepper. Soak roll in water, dry, break up and add. Add mustard or marjoram to taste. Spread the groundmeat mixture on slices of pork. Roll up and tie. Roll in flour, then fry in butter until pleasantly brown on all sides. Add stock or water and simmer 20 to 30 minutes. Remove meat. To the drippings, add more flour and water or stock necessary for gravy. Pour this over pork rolls. Serve with Mashed Potatoes (No. 204) or rice.

Serves 4.

171. Pork Roast *(Schweineschlegel)*

1 6-lb. pork leg (fresh ham)
salt and pepper
1 cup water (more if it
    evaporates)
1 onion
¼ cup butter
2 tbls. flour

Score skin of pork leg lightly in a diamond pattern. Rub with salt and pepper. Bring water to a boil, place in it pork leg and onion. Cover and bake until done (about 4 hours in a 325° oven). Meat must be gray, not pink, throughout. Remove from water. Melt butter and pour over pork. Then, over high heat, crisp the outer skin in the butter. Remove, pour on cold water. Replace in oven to reheat briefly. Prepare gravy from flour and drippings. Serve with Salted Potatoes (No. 199) and Red Cabbage (No. 227) or Brussels Sprouts (No. 224) and Glazed Chestnuts (No. 242).

Serves 4-6.

172. Pork Squares (*Schweinekarree*)

3 lbs. pork loin
salt and pepper
1 cup water
1 onion
1 tomato
1 cup sour cream
1 tbls. flour

Score skin of pork loin lightly in crisscross squares. Season well. Bring water to a boil, place meat, onion and tomato in it. Cover and stew 10 minutes. Remove and roast in a hot (425°) oven about an hour, basting frequently. When done, pour on cream. Slice and arrange on a hot platter. Add flour to pan to make a smooth gravy. Season to taste and strain. Serve with noodles, or potatoes, and a green salad.
Serves 4.

173. Pork and Greens (*Gekochtes Schweinefleisch*)

1 qt. water
6 lbs. spare ribs
soup greens or sauerkraut
salt and pepper

Bring water to a boil. Add meat, soup greens or sauerkraut and seasoning. Stew for about 1½ hours. Serve with any kind of potatoes.
Serves 4.

174. Smoked Ham in Dough (*Schinken in Brotteig*)

1 smoked ham
Mellow Dough, Neutral
(No. 450)

Soak ham overnight in water to cover and remove skin. Or use a ready-to-eat ham and remove skin. Dry well. Prepare dough and wrap it around ham. Bake about three hours in a fairly hot (375°-400°) oven. To serve, cut away crust (with a very sharp knife to prevent crumbling). Slice ham and serve hot or cold, garnished with pieces of the crust.

175. Ham in Madeira or Burgundy
(Schinken in Madeira oder Burgunder)

2 lbs. ham steak
1 onion, chopped
1 tomato, chopped
1 cup Madeira or Burgundy
1 clove
1 bay leaf
1 cup meat stock
2 tbls. flour
2 tbls. butter

Remove rind from ham. Place in a casserole the ham, onion, tomato, wine, seasoning and meat stock and bake in a hot oven (400°) until tender and browned (about ½ hour). Remove from casserole. Add flour, blended with melted butter, to the drippings to prepare a rich gravy, adding extra stock and wine, if desired. Blend well and pour over ham and serve. Serve with Mashed Potatoes (No. 204) or Glazed Chestnuts (No. 242).

Serves 4.

176. Kasseler Roast Ribs of Pork
(Kasseler Rippenspeer)

2-3 lbs. smoked pork
       rib roast
1 onion
1 tomato
1 celery knob, chopped
1 truffle
1 tbls. butter
1 cup water
1 tbls. flour
¼ cup water
¼ cup sour cream
salt and pepper

Scrub the meat, then set in a roasting pan with the onion, tomato, celery, truffle, butter and water. Cover and steam for 1½ hours. When the water has evaporated, turn and brown the meat in the pan fat on all sides. Remove meat and keep it hot. Add flour and water to make gravy, add cream and, if desired, further seasoning. Strain the sauce over the roast and serve. Serve with spring potatoes, sprinkled with chopped parsley, and kale; or Mashed Potatoes (No. 204) and a green salad.

Serves 4-6.

LAMB AND MUTTON (*Hammelfleisch*)

177. Mutton or Lamb Chops (*Hammelkoteletten*)

4-8 mutton or lamb chops
1 clove garlic
1 tbls. oil
salt and pepper
1 onion, sliced
4 tomatoes
1 tbls. flour

Rub chops with garlic, sprinkle with oil and seasonings. With slices of onion and whole tomatoes, broil at high heat for 10-15 minutes. Add flour to drippings and prepare gravy. Lamb chops may also be fried in butter. They should always be crisp on the outside, but a bit rare inside. Serve with Salted Potatoes (No. 199) and green beans.

Serves 4.

178. Mutton Steak (*Hammelsteak*)

1½ lbs. leg of mutton
1 clove garlic
1 tbls. oil
salt and pepper
3 tbls. butter
1 tbls. flour
½ cup water
½ cup claret wine

Carve meat into single portions. Pound and rub with garlic, oil and seasoning. Pre-heat skillet, and over high heat, brown meat on both sides. Add butter, cover and leave over low heat until done, about 30 minutes. Remove to warm platter. To fat in pan, add flour, water and claret to prepare smooth gravy. Serve with Fried Potatoes (No. 200) and beans, peas, or turnips.

Serves 4.

179.   Crown Roast of Lamb *(Lammkrone)*

12-16 chop crown roast of
  lamb
salt and pepper
¼ lb. salt pork
Chestnut Purée (No. 243)

Have the butcher prepare a crown roast with lamb forcemeat in center section. Salt and pepper meat. Cover with wax paper, and to prevent charring, cover rib ends with salt pork and roast in 300° oven for 1¼ hours. To serve, remove pork from rib-ends. On top of forcemeat, fill center with Chestnut Purée.

Serves 6.

180.   Roast Shoulder of Lamb *(Lammrücken)*

4-5 lbs. lamb shoulder
salt and pepper
paprika
2 tbls. butter
2 slices bacon
1 onion, chopped
1 tomato, chopped
1 tbls. flour
¾ cup water
1 cup sour cream

Remove skin but leave fat on shoulder. Season well. Melt butter in a casserole, brown bacon lightly and add the onion, tomato and meat. Cover and roast in 375° oven for 1 to 1½ hours, depending on how well done you like it, basting frequently and adding water, if needed. Remove meat and turn and crisp it under broiler. To the drippings add flour, water and cream to make smooth gravy. Or spread the meat with butter and roast uncovered in oven until all sides are beautifully crisp. When done, pour cream over it and use drippings for gravy. Serve with new potatoes and mixed vegetables or salad.

Serves 4-6.

181. Roast Mutton *(Hammelbraten)*

1 5-lb. leg of mutton
garlic clove
salt and pepper
2 tbls. butter
1 tsp. ginger
1 tomato
1 onion
1 cup water
1 tbls. flour

Rub mutton with garlic, salt and pepper. Fry all sides in butter. Add ginger, tomato, onion and water. Stew, or roast in hot oven for 1½ hours, until done, adding extra water if needed. Crisp meat in pan fat and remove to a hot platter. Add flour and more water to pan and blend well for smooth gravy. Strain and serve. Serve with Potato Dumplings (No. 195). Serves 4-6.

182. Mutton à la Bourgeoise *(Hammel à la Bourgeoise)*

1 onion
3 shallots
3 tbls. butter
2½ lbs. mutton shoulder
½ cup water, hot
pinch of flour
2 tbls. tomato ketchup
1 tbls. olive oil

Chop onion and shallots finely and brown in 1 tablespoon butter. Cut mutton into small pieces, season well, and in a second pan, fry in 2 tablespoons butter 5 minutes over moderate heat. Add browned onion, shallots, hot water, flour and tomato ketchup and cook all together over low heat for about 40 minutes. Before serving, stir in olive oil. Serve with Mashed Potatoes (No. 204). Serves 4.

183. Mutton Ragout à la Bonne Femme
(Hammelragout Bonne Femme)

1 onion
2 tbls. butter
3 lbs. breast or neck of
  mutton
1 bud garlic, chopped
salt and pepper
1 tbls. flour
½ cup water
¼ cup white wine
1 tbls. lemon juice
1 tbls. ketchup or Tomato
  Sauce (No. 284)
½ lb. each carrots, new
  potatoes and green peas

Slice onion and fry lightly in butter to a golden brown. Cut mutton in large cubes, add chopped garlic and seasoning. Add to onions and fry lightly. Sprinkle with flour, add water, wine, lemon juice and Tomato Sauce (or ketchup). Cover and cook 1½ hours. Slice carrots (or cut in strips) and add to stew. Add potatoes and cook another 15 minutes. Add green peas and cook until they are done, about 15 minutes. Serve meat on a hot platter surrounded by vegetables.
Serves 3.

184. Shoulder of Mutton with Turnips
(Hammelschulter mit weissen Rüben)

2 lbs. shoulder of mutton
4 tbls. butter
1 tbls. flour
1¼ cups beef stock
salt and pepper
peppercorns
1 lb. white turnips

Have meat boned, rolled and tied. Heat half the butter and brown meat all around in it. Remove meat and brown flour in the fat. Add beef stock and bring to a boil. Return meat, add seasonings, cover and stew for 2 hours. Meanwhile clean and slice turnips and sauté them in remaining butter until golden brown. Add to meat and continue stewing until fully done, about ½ hour more. Place meat on hot platter, with turnips around it. Strain drippings to use as a sauce. Serve with Salted Potatoes (No. 199).
Serves 4.

GAME (Wildbret)

185. Loin of Venison (Rehrücken)

1 loin of venison, 7 to 9 lbs.
salt and pepper
vinegar, or milk to cover,
    to soak
4 strips of bacon
1 onion, sliced
6 tbls. butter
1 cup beef stock
1 cup sour cream
1 lemon, sliced
2 tbls. flour
1 tsp. lemon juice
1 cup beef stock
1 tsp. cream
½ cup red wine

Deer meat should always be hung in a cool place to age. The longer it ages, the greater its tenderness. One to two weeks is suggested. Ribs, on the loin, may be shortened to give meat a more tractable shape. Rub with salt and pepper, wrap in a cloth soaked in vinegar and store in refrigerator overnight. Or soak overnight in milk. Lard with slivers of bacon, or wrap with sliced bacon. Fry venison, with onion, in butter until slightly brown. Add beef stock, cover and cook over low heat for ¾ hour. Uncover, baste with fat and place in a hot oven (450°) until well browned and crisp, about 15 minutes. Pour on most of the cream and keep in hot oven a little longer. Venison should remain slightly rosy inside. Pour a little of the drippings over the meat and garnish with slices of lemon. Add flour, lemon juice, beef stock, cream and wine to the remaining drippings to prepare a rich gravy, which is served in a separate gravy boat.

Serves 8-10.

186. Venison Fillets (*Rehfilet vom Grill*)

2 lbs. fillet of venison
¼ lb. bacon
salt and pepper
⅓ cup olive oil
cucumber pickles (sour)

Cut fillets into steaks, lard with slivers of bacon, season well. Soak in olive oil, turning and then letting stand for a while so that the oil sinks in. Broil under high heat, 15 minutes on each side until well browned and tender. To serve, garnish with sour pickles. Serve with potatoes or Spätzle (No. 196) and Cumberland Sauce (No. 288).
Serves 3-4.

187. Venison Schnitzel (*Rehschnitzel*)

4 individual steaks or
    cutlets of venison
salt and pepper
4 tbls. butter
2 tomatoes, halved
1 onion, sliced
1 tbls. flour
1 tbls. red wine

Carve steaks from leg of venison. Pound well and season. In a casserole, melt butter, add tomatoes, onion and cutlets. Cook for 10 minutes. Remove meat to a hot platter, garnish with the tomatoes. To fat add flour, more salt and pepper and wine. Strain and serve over meat. Serve with Mashed Potatoes (No. 204), Spätzle (No. 196) or rice.
Serves 4.

188. Leg of Venison *(Rehschlegel)*

½ cup vinegar
1 cup water
1 clove
1 bay leaf
1 onion
salt and pepper
3 lbs. leg of venison
4 tbls. butter
1 tbls. flour
1 tbls. lemon juice
½ cup sour cream
½ cup red wine

Cook the vinegar, water, spices, onion and seasoning for 5 minutes. Pour over meat. Cover and let soak several days. Dry meat and brown in hot butter. Add one cup of the steeping liquid. Simmer, covered, 1½ hours, or roast, uncovered, in a 350° oven. Uncover, turn up heat and crisp meat. Serve on a hot platter. To drippings, add flour, lemon juice, cream and wine to prepare a smooth gravy. Serve with Spätzle (No. 196) and cranberry sauce.
This may be prepared as in No. 185— a less vinegary version.
Serves 4.

189. Rabbit Stew *(Hasenpfeffer)*

Steeping liquid:
½ cup vinegar
½ cup water
1 clove
1 bay leaf
peppercorns
1 onion, sliced
salt and pepper
2 tsp. lemon juice

1 hare or rabbit, cut up,
    with giblets
4 tbls. butter
4 tbls. flour

Cook steeping ingredients together 5 minutes. Pour over meat and let soak for 2 days. Fry briefly in butter, with a little onion. Add flour and let brown. Add ½ cup of steeping liquid, cover and stew until tender, about 1½ hours. If necessary, replenish liquid.
Serves 4.

190. Roast Hare (Hasenbraten)

1 hare or rabbit
2 strips of bacon
salt and pepper
3 tbls. butter
1 onion, chopped
1 cup sour cream
½ lemon, sliced
1 tbls. flour
seasoning to taste
½ lemon, juice

Lard meat with slivers of bacon or wrap bacon around pieces. Season well. Melt butter, turn meat in it. Add onion, cover and roast in a hot (400°) oven for 30 minutes, basting frequently. After 20 minutes, pour on sour cream. Remove meat, when done, to a warm platter. Garnish with lemon slices. To fat add flour, seasonings and lemon juice. Blend and heat thoroughly. Serve in a gravy boat. Serve with Spätzle (No. 196), cabbage and cranberry sauce.
Serves 4.

DUMPLINGS *(Klösse und Knödel)*

191. Bavarian Bread Dumplings
(Bayerische Semmelklösse)

10 white rolls
1-2 cups milk
½ cup bacon or ham
1 tbls. butter
1 small onion, chopped
1 tbls. parsley, chopped
3 eggs
salt and pepper
nutmeg

Slice rolls finely and soak in lukewarm milk. Bread should be moist but not soggy. Dice bacon or ham and fry in butter together with chopped onion and parsley. Add eggs and seasoning to bread slices and combine with fried ingredients. Shape into dumplings. Cook in salt water for 20 minutes. Serve immediately.
Serves 4.

192. Bread Dumplings Without Egg (*Semmelklösse ohne Ei*)

8 white rolls
1 cup semolina
1 tbls. butter
salt
nutmeg
½ cup salted water, hot

Chop rolls finely and mix with semolina and melted butter. Season to taste. Add water slowly and blend in to proper consistency. Wet hands and shape mixture into dumplings. Cook in salted water 15 to 20 minutes. Serve immediately. Serves 4.

193. Tyrolean Dumplings (*Tiroler Knödel*)

4 slices of bread
½ cup bacon fat
1½ cups flour
1 cup milk
1 egg
1 egg yolk
½ tsp. basil
1 tsp. parsley, chopped
salt and pepper

Remove crusts from bread and cube it. Add bread to bacon fat and let it absorb fat completely. Store in a deep bowl to cool. Mix well the flour, milk and eggs. Add seasoning and pour this mixture over bread cubes. Let stand 15 minutes, to absorb liquid fully. Stir gently for thorough blending. Flour hands and knead dough. Shape into dumplings. Cook in salted water for 15 minutes, covered, over low heat. Serves 4.

194. Bohemian Dumplings (*Böhmische Knödel*)

2 cups flour
2 eggs
1 cup milk
salt
nutmeg
2 rolls
1 tbls. fat

Mix flour, eggs, milk and seasoning in a bowl. Beat until it blisters. Dice rolls finely; fry lightly in fat and mix into dough. If dough seems thin, add flour to achieve firm but pliable consistency. Scoop out tablespoon-size dumplings and let simmer in salted water for 15 to 20 minutes. Serves 4.

195. Potato Dumplings (*Gekochte Kartoffelklosse*)

2 lbs. potatoes
2 cups flour
2 eggs
salt
nutmeg
2 slices bread
1 tbls. butter

Cook potatoes the day before in their skins. Next day peel and mash potatoes. Add flour, eggs and seasoning and knead to a firm dough. Cube bread and fry lightly in butter. Shape dumplings, bore a hole in each and put in several fried bread cubes. Close over the hole. Drop into boiling salted water and cook 10 to 15 minutes. Try one test dumpling in the water; if it falls apart, work more flour into the dough.
Serves 4.

196. Spätzle

4 cups flour
3 eggs
1 cup water
1 tbls. salt

Prepare a firm dough from the flour, eggs, water and salt. Beat until it comes easily away from the sides of the bowl. Form dumplings and cook in boiling salted water. Skim them out, dip in cold water and serve on a hot platter. Spätzle may also be browned lightly in butter before serving. A favorite accompaniment to meat and vegetables.
Serves 4.

197. Cheese Spätzle (*Käsespätzle*)

Spätzle (No. 196)
grated cheese

Prepare Spätzle, tumble in grated cheese and serve on a hot platter with Onion Butter (No. 296).
Serves 4.

POTATOES *(Kartoffelgerichte)*

198. Potatoes in Their Jackets
(Kartoffeln in der Schale)

8 medium potatoes
1 tsp. caraway seeds
1 tsp. salt

Brush potatoes clean in cold water. Change water and cook together with caraway seeds and salt for 30 minutes. Test with fork to be sure they are done. Drain off water. Replace pot over low heat and systematically shake it so potatoes will dry.
Serves 4.

199. Salted Potatoes *(Salzkartoffeln)*

2 lbs. potatoes
1 tbls. salt

Peel raw potatoes and cut in wedges. Place in cold salted water. Cover and cook until done, about 20 minutes. Drain immediately to prevent crumbling. Replace in pot and shake around, over low heat, to dry. Serve sprinkled with parsley or topped with Melted Butter (No. 294) or Onion Butter (No. 296).
Serves 4-6.

200. Fried Potatoes, Raw *(Bratkartoffeln, roh)*

8 medium potatoes
2 tbls. butter
1 onion, chopped
salt and pepper
½ cup water

Peel the potatoes and slice thinly. In skillet brown onions in butter. Add potatoes and season well. Turn over often with spatula to avoid sticking. Add water, cover and stew over low heat until done, about 20 minutes.
Serves 4.

201. Niedernauer Potatoes
(Niedernauer Kartoffeln)

2½ lbs. potatoes, cooked
2 tsp. butter
salt and pepper
4 tbls. sour cream
1 egg
parsley

Peel cold cooked potatoes and cut into small cubes. Fry in melted butter, adding seasoning to taste. Mix cream and egg and pour over potatoes. Let cook until thickened. Serve garnished with parsley. Serves 6.

202. Fish Potatoes (Fischkartoffeln)

2 lbs. large potatoes
water to cover
1 tsp. salt
2 tbls. butter
salt and pepper
1 tbls. parsley, chopped

Peel raw potatoes, and with a special cutter, cut out marble-sized balls. Cook until tender in salted water. Turn in melted butter, season and serve garnished with parsley.
Note: This makes an attractive side dish for all sorts of fish. There is no other reason for the name.
Serves 6.

203. Devonshire Fried Potatoes
(Devonshire Bratkartoffeln)

4 large potatoes
salt and pepper
2 large onions
4 tbls. butter

Cook unpeeled potatoes until done; peel while still hot and mash. Add seasoning. Slice onions thinly and fry in butter until golden-brown. Mix potatoes and onions together and add more seasoning. Spread 2 inches deep in a buttered baking dish, dot with more butter and bake 15 to 20 minutes in a moderate (350°) oven.
Serves 4.

204. Mashed Potatoes (*Kartoffelpüree*)

6 medium potatoes
2 cups milk
2 tbls. butter
salt
Onion Butter (No. 296)

Cook unpeeled potatoes, peel while still hot and mash. Heat milk lukewarm, add potatoes, butter and salt and beat until smooth. Serve on hot platter. Dent the surface with the back of a spoon (like footprint) and fill with Onion Butter. Serves 6.

205. Buttered Potatoes (*Butterkartoffeln*)

4 large potatoes
4 tbls. butter
salt

Select not too mealy potatoes. Peel and cut into wedges or thick slices. Melt butter, add potatoes and cook over low heat. Turn over several times, adding more butter if needed. (Be careful that the potatoes do not fall to pieces in this process.) When nearly done, increase heat and add salt to taste. The finished potatoes should be golden brown on the outside, smooth and creamy on the inside. Serves 4.

206. Alsatian Fried Potatoes (*Pommes frites*)

4 large potatoes
fat, to cover
salt, to taste

Pare raw potatoes and cut lengthwise in strips ½ inch thick. Dry thoroughly in a towel. Fry small quantities at a time in hot deep fat, using a spatula to keep pieces from sticking together. When potatoes are golden brown, remove to strainer to drain, then sprinkle with salt. *Note:* When preparing large quantities, the small initial lots may be fried lightly and stored in a strainer. Finish larger lots as above, in deep fat. It is practical to use a wire French fryer. Serves 4.

207. Potato Nests (*Kartoffelnester*)

6 potatoes
deep fat
salt, to taste

Pare raw potatoes and cut in long, thin, winding ribbons. Soak 15 minutes in cold water, then dry thoroughly in a towel. Place in a wire strainer, a few at a time, and fry in deep, moderately hot fat until browned. Carefully remove from strainer, dry on absorbent paper, sprinkle with salt. Coil into nests and top with small fillets of fried fish or vegetables.
Serves 6.

208. Potato Fondant (*Pommes fondant*)

3½ cups cooked potatoes, mashed
3 tbls. butter
1½ tsp. salt
dash of pepper
¼ tsp. parsley, chopped
⅔ cup milk, hot
½ cup sweet cream
¼ cup bread crumbs

Mix mashed potatoes, while still hot, with butter, salt, pepper, parsley and hot milk. Beat thoroughly for 3 minutes. Turn into a buttered baking dish. Pour cream over mixture and sprinkle with bread crumbs. Bake in hot (425°) oven until crumbs are well browned.
Serves 6.

209. Sweet Potatoes, Southern Style (*Süsskartoffeln, südliche Art*)

6 medium sweet potatoes
2 tbls. butter
½ cup sweet cream
salt
¼ cup sherry

Bake whole sweet potatoes in oven until done, 30 to 40 minutes. Cut lengthwise and scoop out insides. Mash this and mix with butter, cream, salt and sherry. Stuff back in shells and bake for 5 minutes in hot (450°) oven.
Serves 6.

210. Sweet Potatoes, Baked Over (Süsskartoffeln, überbacken)

6 sweet potatoes, cooked
salt and pepper
6 tbls. brown sugar
3 tbls. butter
3 tbls. bread crumbs

Slice cooked sweet potatoes ½ inch thick. Place in layers in a buttered baking dish, sprinkling each layer with salt, pepper, brown sugar and butter. Cover the top layer with buttered bread crumbs and bake in hot (450°) oven until well browned, about 20 minutes. Serves 6.

211. Creamed Potatoes (Rahmkartoffeln)

6 potatoes
2 tbls. butter
3 tbls. flour
1 cup cream
1 tbls. parsley, chopped
nutmeg, to taste
salt and pepper

Select firm potatoes. Cook until tender. Peel and slice fairly thick. Melt butter, add flour, cream, parsley and seasoning. Heat potatoes thoroughly in this sauce. Recipe may be varied by substituting grated cheese for parsley. Serves 4-6.

212. Potato Puffs (Kartoffelpuffer, Reibekuchen)

4 large potatoes
2 eggs
1 cup milk
3 tbls. flour
salt
1 tbls. fat
sugar, if desired

Pare and grate raw potatoes. Drain off liquid. Mix with eggs, milk, flour and salt to form a firm dough. Heat fat in skillet Put dough in skillet, 2 tablespoons at a time, and spread out thinly to form small pancakes. Fry on both sides to a rich golden brown. Sprinkle with either salt or sugar and serve hot. Serves 4.

213. Potato Noodles *(Schupfnudeln)*

4 large potatoes
1 egg
2 cups flour
salt
nutmeg
butter for frying or topping
bread crumbs

Cook and peel potatoes, and mash. Mix with egg, flour and seasoning. On a floured bread board, work into a firm dough, adding extra flour if needed. Shape dough into large rolls. Slice rolls, then slice these slices into the thinnest possible ribbons, or noodles. Cook noodles in salted water until they float to the surface. Drain, fry briefly in hot fat. Or serve topped with browned butter and bread crumbs.

Serves 4.

214. Potato Croquettes *(Kartoffelkroketten)*

4 large potatoes
3 tbls. butter
1 egg (whole)
1 egg, separated
salt
nutmeg
flour, as needed
1 cup bread crumbs
deep fat

Cook potatoes, peel while hot, and grate. Melt butter over low heat. Mix with potatoes, egg and egg yolk, and seasoning. Let batter stand to cool. Flour a bread board, turn out batter and form into patties, adding flour if needed. Beat egg white, dip patties in it, then in bread crumbs. Fry in deep fat until well browned.

Serves 4.

VEGETABLES *(Gemüse)*

215. Young Vegetables *(Junges Gemüse)*

1 lb. assorted young vegetables, such as peas, carrots, string beans, cauliflower, etc.
salt
2 tbls. butter
1 tbls. parsley, chopped
¼ tsp. pepper
1 tbls. butter
1 tbls. flour
1 cup cooking water or
cooking water and cream

Wash vegetables and cook in just enough salted water to cover, but do not let it evaporate. When done, drain and save water; tumble vegetables in butter and sprinkle with parsley and pepper. Prepare sauce with butter, flour, cooking water, or cooking water blended with cream. Cooking water may also be used as a soup base.
Serves 2.

216. Asparagus *(Spargel)*

2 lbs. asparagus
salt
2 tbls. bread crumbs in 4 tbls.
butter or Hollandaise
Sauce (No. 272) or Sauce
Vinaigrette (No. 289)

Clean fresh asparagus and remove hard end of stems. Bundle together and cut to assure even length. Set in lightly salted boiling water and cook until done, about 20 to 25 minutes. Asparagus is done if it bends when lifted out of water. Drain well (saving liquid) and serve on a hot platter. Cover with bread crumbs browned in butter or with Hollandaise Sauce or Sauce Vinaigrette. The cooking water may be used as a soup base or, cool, as a wholesome vegetable juice drink. In the latter case, do not salt too heavily.
Serves 2-4.

217.   Spinach (Spinat)

1 lb. spinach
¼ tsp. salt, in water to cover
pinch of baking soda
2 tbls. butter
1 tbls. flour
1 cup or more water or milk
cream
¼ bud garlic, crushed
salt and pepper

Wash spinach thoroughly and drop into boiling water. Add a dash of baking soda. Bring again to a boil and cook briefly, about 3 to 5 minutes. It is very important not to overcook spinach, as it turns brown and bitter. Strain off liquid and put spinach through a sieve. Prepare a light sauce with butter, flour, a little of the cooking water or milk. Add cream to desired consistency. Season and serve. Serves 2.

218.   Baked Cauliflower (Blumenkohl, überbacken)

1 medium head cauliflower
1 tsp. salt in water to cover
Butter Sauce (No. 268)
1 tbls. bread crumbs
1 tbls. cheese, grated
3 tbls. butter (to grease dish
    and dot)

Wash cauliflower and drop into boiling salted water. Cook until nearly done, about 20 minutes. Put it through a sieve and into a buttered baking dish. Cover with sauce, bread crumbs and cheese. Dot with butter. Bake in moderate oven (350°) until nicely browned. Serves 4.

219.   Cauliflower, Polish Style (Blumenkohl, polnisch)

1 head cauliflower
salt, in water to cover
2 egg yolks
3 tbls. butter
1 tbls. bread crumbs.

Divide cauliflower into several medium-sized sections and soak in cold salted water for 15 minutes. Bring water to a boil and cook cauliflower in it until tender, about 10 minutes. Drain and remove carefully so vegetable will not break up. Put on a hot platter. Beat egg yolks and pour over cauliflower. Melt butter and brown bread crumbs lightly in it. Top cauliflower with this and serve. Serves 4.

220. Lima Beans *(Puffbohnen)*

1 lb. lima beans
milk, to cover
salt and pepper
parsley, chopped
2 tbls. butter

Cover shelled beans with milk and cook until tender. Season well, sprinkle with parsley and tumble in melted butter. Serve with sliced ham.

Serves 2-3

221. Casserole Baked Beans *(Bohnenkerne)*

1 lb. dried peas or beans
dash of salt
1 bay leaf
4 medium tomatoes, sliced
4 strips bacon
1 onion, sliced
¼ cup cheese, grated

Soak dried peas or navy beans overnight. Cook in salted water, together with bay leaf, until soft, 2 to 3 hours. Arrange alternating layers of beans, sliced tomatoes, lightly fried bacon and sliced onions in a buttered casserole. Top with grated cheese, dot with butter and bake in hot (400°) oven until nicely browned, about 20 minutes.

Serves 4.

222. Kohlrabi

4 kohlrabi
1 tsp. salt
pinch of baking soda
2 tbls. butter
1 tbls. flour
1 cup beef stock
salt, pepper, nutmeg to taste
1 tbls. chopped parsley
2 tbls. cream

Remove tender leaves from stalks and cook in salted water with a pinch of baking soda. Rinse in cold water, drain well and chop finely. Pare and slice the tubers. Cook in lightly salted water until done, 25 to 30 minutes. Prepare a light sauce from butter, flour, beef stock, seasonings and cream. Add sliced kohlrabi and bring to a boil again. Either add chopped, cooked greens to this or serve separately, with greens surrounding tubers.

Serves 4.

223. Cucumber Vegetable *(Gurkengemüse)*

2 medium cucumbers
4 tomatoes
salt, pepper, dill (chopped)
3 tbls. butter
lemon juice or vinegar

Pare cucumbers, cutting toward stem end. Chop up cucumbers and tomatoes. Season well and sauté in butter. Before serving, add a dash of lemon juice or vinegar.
Serves 4.

224. Brussels Sprouts *(Rosenkohl)*

1 lb. Brussels sprouts
salt, baking soda
1 tbls. butter
1 tbls. flour
¼ cup cooking water
3 tbls. cream or milk
salt and pepper
nutmeg

Cook sprouts in slightly salted water with a pinch of baking soda for 10 to 20 minutes. Prepare a sauce with butter, flour, cooking water, cream or milk and seasoning. Add sprouts and bring to a boil again.
Serves 4.

225. Curly Cabbage *(Wirsing)*

2 lbs. cabbage
salt, baking soda
1 small onion, chopped
1 tsp. parsley, chopped
2 tbls. butter
2 tbls. flour
1 cup beef stock or milk
salt and pepper
nutmeg
extra butter and cream, as
 desired

Divide up cabbage and remove stalk and ribs. Soak in strongly salted water. Rinse. Cook in slightly salted water, with a pinch of baking soda, until nearly done, about 10 minutes. Drain thoroughly and put through grinder. Brown onion and parsley lightly in butter. Add flour, stir in beef stock or milk and cook briefly. Add cabbage and seasoning and heat through. This can be further enriched by adding extra butter or a little cream.
Variation: Remove and wash outer leaves and cook briefly in salted water. Drain, top with bread crumbs browned in butter, and serve immediately. Brussels sprouts may also be prepared in this way.
Serves 4.

226. Bavarian Cabbage *(Bayerisches Kraut)*

2 lbs. cabbage
1 apple
2 tbls. butter
1 bay leaf
salt and pepper
juniper berries
1 tbls. flour
½ cup white wine
sugar
vinegar

Wash and shred cabbage. Slice apple. Melt butter in pan and add cabbage and apple. Mix thoroughly. Season well with bay leaf, salt, pepper and a few juniper berries. Cook in one cup of water, more if needed, over low heat until done, about 10 minutes. When liquid has evaporated, sprinkle with flour, add wine and sugar and vinegar to taste. Serve immediately. Serves 4.

227. Red Cabbage *(Rotkraut)*

2 lbs. red cabbage
1 apple
2 tbls. butter
1 bay leaf
salt and pepper
juniper berries
1 tbls. flour
½ cup red wine
1 tsp. apple or juniper jelly
1-2 cloves

Prepare like Bavarian Cabbage, No. 226, but use red instead of white wine and, to taste, add apple or juniper jelly and cloves instead of sugar and vinegar. Serves 4.

228. Winter Cabbage *(Winterkohl)*

2 lbs. cabbage
salt, baking soda
2 tbls. flour
1 small onion, chopped
2 tbls. butter
1 cup beef stock
salt and pepper

This is cabbage gathered after the first frost. Remove any yellow leaves and stalks and wash well. Cook 8 minutes in boiling salted water with a pinch of baking soda. Rinse in cold water and grind, or chop finely. Brown flour and onion in butter, add beef stock and cook about 5 minutes. Add chopped cabbage and seasoning and cook again briefly. Overcooking will make cabbage bitter and unattractive. Serves 4.

229. Leeks *(Lauchgemüse)*

6 leeks
½ tsp. salt in water to cover
2 tbls. butter
2 tbls. flour
½ cup milk
½ cup (or more) cooking
    water
salt and pepper
nutmeg
2 tbls. cream

Remove green parts from stalks, cut the rest in finger-thick slices and grate. Cook 10 minutes in boiling salted water. Drain, reserving water. Prepare a light sauce from butter, flour and milk, thin with vegetable water to desired consistency, and season. Add leeks to sauce and heat through. Add cream and serve hot.
Serves 4.

230. Mushrooms *(Pilze)*

2 lbs. mushrooms
2 tbls. olive oil
2 tbls. butter
1 small onion, chopped
salt and pepper
parsley

Clean mushrooms carefully. Fry them lightly, 3 minutes, in olive oil. Add butter, onion, salt and pepper. Cover and let simmer for 10 minutes. Garnish with parsley to serve.
Variation: Cook mushrooms until tender, sprinkle with flour and enrich the liquid with milk.
Serves 4.

231. Egg Plant *(Auberginen oder Eierfrüchte)*

2 small eggplants
salt
flour
3 tbls. butter
½ cup cheese, grated
1 cup Tomato Sauce
(No. 284)
½ cup bread crumbs
butter, to dot
salt and pepper

Peel eggplants and cut into ¼-inch slices. Salt lightly, dip in flour and fry lightly on both sides in butter. Grease a baking dish. Place slices in this and add part of the cheese, the Tomato Sauce and seasoning. Sprinkle with bread crumbs, and again with cheese. Dot with butter. Bake in moderate (325°) oven for 20 minutes, or until nicely browned.

Variation: Peel eggplant and hollow out. Soak 10 minutes in a marinade of olive oil and lemon juice. Remove from marinade. Stuff with chopped leftover meat, sprinkle with grated cheese, dot with butter and bake in 350° oven until done, about 30 minutes. Serve with Tomato Sauce. The hollowed-out insides can be fried lightly, combined with stewed tomatoes and baked for a subsequent meal. Serves 2-4.

232. Artichokes *(Artischocken)*

2-4 artichokes
salt

Trim off stems of artichokes and also the hard tips of the leaves. Cook in boiling salted water 30 to 40 minutes. When done, leaves pull out easily. Serve in a napkin. Serve with Hollandaise Sauce (No. 272) Mousseline Sauce (No. 274) or Sauce Vinaigrette (No. 289). Serves 2-4.

233. Oporto Onions *(Oportozweibeln)*

4 large onions
salted water or beef stock,
   to cover
3 tbls. butter

Remove outer skin of onions. Cook in salted water or beef stock about 40 minutes. Pour on melted butter to serve. *Variation:* Cook 4 large onions 20 minutes. Halve, hollow out and stuff with chopped meat. Place in greased baking dish. Add 1 cup beef stock. Sprinkle with grated cheese, dot with butter and bake in 400° oven until well browned, 20 to 25 minutes. The insides of onions may be sliced and fried for a subsequent meal.
Serves 4.

234. Onions *(Zweibeln)*

1 lb. small onions
1 tbls. sugar
2 tbls. butter
¼ cup gravy or beef stock
salt and pepper

Remove outer skin. Cook in salted water 15 minutes and drain well. Brown sugar and butter in a skillet and turn onions in this. Add gravy or beef stock and seasoning. Brown and glaze the onions over strong heat, turning constantly. This makes an excellent side dish for Pork Chops (No. 165) and Glazed Chestnuts (No. 242). Celery, carrots and turnips may be prepared in this same way.
Serves 2-4.

235. Chicory *(Chicorée)*

1 head chicory
salted water, to cover
butter, for baking dish
juice of 1 lemon
salt and pepper
gravy or cream

Remove any wilted leaves and the stalks. Cook 5 minutes in salted water. Rinse in cold water. Place in a greased baking dish, sprinkle with lemon juice, salt and pepper and add gravy or cream to cover. Cover with wax paper and bake in moderate (350°) oven until well done, about 25 minutes.
Serves 4.

236. Turnips *(Teltower Rübchen)*

2 lbs. small turnips
1 tsp. salt in water to cover
1 tbls. sugar
2 tbls. butter
1 tbls. flour
1-2 cups cooking water
salt and pepper

Scrape turnips to clean. Cook in salted water until half-done, 10 to 15 minutes; save liquid. Brown sugar in butter and tumble turnips in this. Add flour and cooking water. Cover and stew over low heat until tender, about 30 minutes. Season to taste and serve with lamb or pork roasts.
Serves 6.

237. Red Beets in Butter *(Rote Rüben in Butter)*

1¼ lbs. beets, cooked
3 tbls. butter
1 tsp. parsley, chopped
1 tsp. chives, chopped
¼ section garlic
1 tsp. flour
1 tbls. vinegar
salt and pepper

Peel and slice beets. Melt butter in stew pan and add parsley, chives and garlic. Sprinkle lightly with flour and let simmer. Add beets, vinegar and seasoning and simmer for another 30 minutes. Serve with Mashed Potatoes (No. 204).
Serves 4.

238. Sauerkraut

2 lbs. cabbage
3 tbls. butter
1 onion, chopped
apple, sliced
salt and pepper
1 potato, raw
½ cup white wine

Pluck apart cabbage and wash well. Shred. Melt butter in a fairly large pot and turn cabbage in it thoroughly. Add onion, apple and seasoning to taste. Fill pot with water. Cook until tender, about 10 minutes. Grate into this raw potato, to give a nice texture. Add wine before serving.

Variation: Instead of wine, paprika, sugar and cream may be used to season. Or champagne may be substituted for white wine. This last is particularly good when served with venison or pheasant.

Serves 4.

239. Celery (*Sellerie*)

2 celery knobs
2 cups water, salted, or 2
    cups beef stock
2 tbls. butter
1 tbls. flour
¼ cup cream or milk
salt and pepper
1 egg yolk, beaten

Cut up celery knobs and cook until tender in either salted water or beef stock. Prepare a sauce with butter, flour, milk or cream and seasoning. Heat celery thoroughly in this. Just before serving, thicken with egg yolk.

Serves 2.

240. Dried Lentils, Peas, Beans (*Hülsenfrüchte*)

½ lb. lentils, peas or beans
dash of baking soda
2 tbls. pork fat
2 tbls. flour
salt, pepper and (with lentils)
    dash of vinegar
marjoram, if peas
garlic, if beans

Soak the legumes overnight in cold water. Next day change water, add baking soda and cook until well done, 2 to 3 hours, adding water to keep beans covered. Prepare a marinade with all other ingredients and thin with cooking water. Add lentils, peas or beans, season to taste, and once more heat thoroughly.

Serves 3-4.

241. Purée of Dried Green Peas (*Erbsenpüree*)

1 lb. peas, dried
dash baking soda
2 tbls. pork fat
2 tbls. flour
salt and pepper
Onion Butter

Soak peas overnight. Drain and cook in fresh water with baking soda until tender, 2 to 3 hours. Put through strainer. For flavor and thickening, and before serving, melt the fat salt pork, brown flour in it and add to the purée. If too thick, add additional cooking water. Serve with Onion Butter (No. 296).
Serves 4.

242. Glazed Chestnuts (*Glasierte Kastanien*)

1 lb. chestnuts
1 tbls. sugar
1 tbls. butter
2 tbls. beef gravy
beef stock or water
salt

Rub chestnuts with oil and bake in oven until shells crack. Shell and soak in water until skin loosens. Peel. Lightly brown sugar and butter and turn chestnuts in this mixture. Add gravy and enough beef stock (or water) to cover. Season to taste. Cover and steam until chestnuts are tender and glazed.
Serves 4-6.

243. Chestnut Purée (*Kastanienpüree*)

1¼ lbs. chestnuts
2 cups milk
5 tbls. butter
salt
1 tsp. sugar

Shell chestnuts and soak in boiling water until skin peels off. Cook in milk until tender. Drain, reserving milk. Mash chestnuts, salt and sugar and return to cooking milk, adding more milk if necessary, and bring to a boil.
Serves 4.

SALADS AND DRESSINGS
(Salate und Marinaden)

244. Cucumber Salad (Gurkensalat)

2 large cucumbers
3 tbls. olive oil or ¼ cup
    sour cream
2 tbls. vinegar
1 tbls. water
parsley
salt and pepper

Peel cucumbers, cutting toward the stem end. Slice very thinly, add and blend oil or cream. Add other ingredients immediately before serving.
Serves 4.

245. Endive or Chicory Salad with Oranges
(Endiven oder Chicoréesalat mit Orangen)

2 large Belgian endives
1 orange, seedless
¼ cup sweet cream
1 tbls. mustard
salt and pepper

Remove outer leaves, using only those that are white. Cut leaves in half, along center. Place on platter. Peel oranges, removing inner white skin. Shred peels and cook for 5 minutes to eliminate any bitterness. Dry and cool. Mix cream with mustard, salt and pepper and pour this marinade over endive. Sprinkle with shredded orange peels. Slice remainder of orange and garnish salad with orange slices. (Chicory may be substituted for the endive.)
Serves 4.

246. Cucumber Baskets (*Gurkenkörbchen*)

3 large cucumbers
3 tomatoes
salad dressing
lettuce leaves

Without paring cucumbers, cut off each end squarely. Cut in half. Scoop out insides and dice. Chop up tomatoes. Add salad dressing to cucumber and tomato mixture and blend well. Fill each half. Set upright and serve on lettuce leaves. Serves 6.

247. Bolivian Salad (*Bolivianischer Salat*)

1½ cups cooked potatoes, diced
3 eggs, hard-cooked and chopped
1½ tbls. red peppers, chopped
½ tbls. chives, chopped
Cream Dressing (No. 267)
lettuce leaves

Mix cold potatoes with hard-cooked eggs, red peppers and chives. Pour dressing over this and serve on nests of lettuce. Serves 6.

248. Banana Salad (*Bananensalat*)

4 bananas
French Dressing (No. 264)
¼ head of lettuce

Strip off one section of the peel of each banana. Scoop out the fruit. Slice thinly contents of one banana, chop up remainder. Mix chopped-up banana with dressing and refill open shells. Decorate with the slices. Serve on lettuce. Serves 4.

249. Radish Salad (*Rettichsalat*)

2 bunches red radishes
1 tbls. olive oil
2 tbls. vinegar
1 tsp. chives, chopped
salt and pepper
¼ cup sour cream, optional

Wash radishes and slice or grate them. Sprinkle with salt and let stand for 5 minutes. Mix oil, vinegar, chives and seasoning to form a marinade, pour over radishes and let stand. If desired, add sour cream immediately before serving.
Serves 4.

250. Bean Salad (*Bohnensalat*)

1 lb. green beans
3 tbls. olive oil
3 tbls. vinegar
3 tbls. beef stock
1 onion, sliced
pinch of dill
salt and pepper

Slice beans lengthwise and cut in half. Cook in salted water until tender. Prepare marinade of remaining ingredients. Pour over beans and let soak in well. Additional beef stock may be added for extra juiciness.
Serves 4.

251. Dried Bean Salad (*Kernbohnensalat*)

½ lb. dried white beans
3 tbls. vinegar
3 tbls. water
1 cup beef stock
salt and pepper
1 bud garlic, crushed
1-2 strips bacon

Wash beans and let soak in water overnight. Next day, cook until tender, about 2 to 3 hours. From the remaining ingredients, except bacon, prepare a marinade. Pour this over the beans and let soak in well. Chop bacon and fry to a light brown. Just before serving, pour bacon grease and chopped bacon over beans.
Serves 4.

252. Celery Salad (*Selleriesalat*)

2 large celery knobs
3 tbls. vinegar
3 tbls. olive oil
1 cup beef stock
1 small onion, chopped
salt and pepper

Scrape celery and cook in salted water until tender. Chop up. Prepare marinade from the other ingredients, mix well with celery and let stand for several hours. Instead of olive oil, one or two strips of bacon, chopped and lightly browned, with the bacon fat may be used. This should be added to the salad at the last minute.
Serves 4.

253. Mushroom Salad (*Pilzsalat*)

½ lb. French mushrooms
2 tbls. oil
1 tbls. vinegar or
    lemon juice
1 tbls. water
salt and pepper
parsley, chopped
onions or pickles, as desired

Cook mushrooms, either whole or sliced, for 4 to 5 minutes in boiling salted water. Mix oil, vinegar, water and seasonings well for a smooth marinade. Pour over mushrooms and let soak thoroughly. Garnish with chopped parsley, little onions or pickles, to serve.
Serves 2.

254. Red Beet Salad (*Rote Rübensalat*)

1 lb. red beets
4 tbls. vinegar
4 tbls. water
½ tsp. sugar
2 tsp. caraway seeds
1 small onion, chopped
1 tsp. cloves, ground
1 bay leaf
salt and pepper
3-4 tbls. olive oil

Scrub beets and cook in salted water until tender. Dip in cold water, peel and slice thinly. From other ingredients, prepare a marinade, smoothing it out with oil to taste. Pour marinade over beets and let soak for several hours.
Serves 4.

255. Cabbage Salad (*Krautsalat*)

1 medium head of red or
   white cabbage
3 tbls. oil or 2 strips of
   bacon, chopped
½ cup vinegar
½ cup water
salt and pepper
caraway seeds

Shred cabbage as finely as possible. Soak for 10 minutes in boiling water. Drain. Prepare a marinade with oil and seasoning and let cabbage soak in this for an hour or more. If bacon is substituted for oil, prepare marinade from vinegar, water and seasoning. Fry bacon lightly and add bacon and fat, while still hot, just before serving.
Serves 4.

256. Sauerkraut Salad (*Sauerkrautsalat*)

½ lb. prepared sauerkraut
3 tbls. olive oil
2 apples, grated
1 onion, chopped
1 tsp. sugar
salt and pepper

Drain sauerkraut. Make marinade of other ingredients and add. Let stand 15 minutes before serving. This salad goes particularly well with fish.
Serves 4.

257. Danish Salad (*Dänischer Salat*)

½ lb. green peas
¼ lb. macaroni
1 cup mayonnaise
1 tbls. parsley, chopped

Cook peas and macaroni separately in boiling water until tender. Drain and cool. Cut macaroni in inch-long pieces and add peas. Mix well with mayonnaise. Sprinkle with chopped parsley.
Serves 4.

258. Potato Salad (Kartoffelsalat)

2 lbs. potatoes
4 tbls. olive oil or bacon fat
2 tbls. vinegar
1 cup beef stock
1 small onion, chopped
salt and pepper

Select good firm potatoes. Cook until tender. Peel and slice. When cool, sprinkle with oil or bacon fat and vinegar; add beef stock, onion and seasoning. Mix carefully and let stand overnight or for several hours. Before serving add a dash of pepper and a few drops of olive oil or beef stock.
Serves 4.

259. Cauliflower Salad (Blumenkohlsalat)

1 head cauliflower
water to cover
1 tsp. salt
3 tbls. olive oil
4 tbls. soup stock
2 tbls. vinegar
salt and pepper

Cook whole head of cauliflower in salted water until nearly done. Drain. Break up into little bouquets. Prepare marinade of other ingredients and mix in with bouquets. Allow to soak in thoroughly. Or cauliflower may be cooked in water to which vinegar and seasoning have been added, broken into bouquets and topped with mayonnaise.
Serves 4.

260. Theatre Salad (Theatersalat)

1 cup fillets of salt herring
1 cup cooked potatoes, diced
1 hard-cooked egg, chopped
French Dressing (No. 264)
¼ cup whipping cream
2 tbls. pimento paste
2 tbls. mayonnaise
lettuce leaves

Cook salt herring for 15 minutes in boiling water. Drain, cool and flake. Mix well with diced potatoes and chopped egg. Cover with dressing and let soak for an hour. Whip cream and fold in pimento. Mix with mayonnaise. Pour over salad and serve on nests of lettuce.
Serves 4.

261.   Chicken Salad (*Hühnersalat*)

2 cups cooked chicken,
    boned and diced
1½ cups celery, chopped
1 cup sweet cream
lettuce leaves
capers
pickles or tomato ketchup

Mix chicken and celery and tumble in cream. Arrange on lettuce. Garnish with capers, finely sliced pickles or dash of ketchup.

Serves 2.

262.   Fish Salad (*Fischsalat*)

2 cups cooked fish, flaked
3 tbls. cream
1 tbls. vinegar or lemon
    juice
beef stock, to proper
    consistency
1 tbls. mustard, prepared
salt and pepper
lemon slices
parsley

Prepare marinade from all other ingredients and add fish. Let soak well and serve garnished with lemon slices and parsley.

Serves 2.

263.   Ox Tongue Salad (*Ochsenmaulsalat*)

1 ox tongue
3 tbls. olive oil
3 tbls. vinegar
¼ cup water
1 onion, chopped
peppercorns
salt and pepper

Wash tongue and cook in salted water until tender, about 3 hours. Cool and slice thinly. Prepare marinade from all other ingredients and let slices of tongue soak in it until ready to serve. Marinade may be poured off and served as extra sauce.

Serves 4.

SALAD DRESSINGS

264. French Dressing
(Französische Rahmmarinade)

½ tsp. salt
¼ tsp. pepper
2 tbls. lemon juice
4 tbls. olive oil
3 tbls. sweet cream

Combine all ingredients, in order given, and mix well. Serve with green, meat or vegetable salad.

265. Club Dressing (Clubmarinade)

2 tbls. olive oil
2 tbls. vinegar
2 tbls. cognac
½ tsp. salt
¼ tsp. pepper

Mix all ingredients well. Serve with lettuce, fruit or meat salad.

266. Rhineland Dressing (Rhineland Marinade)

1 tbls. powdered sugar
2 tsp. Worcestershire sauce
2 tsp. tomato ketchup
1½ tbls. vinegar
1 tbls. olive oil
½ tsp. salt
¼ tsp. mustard, prepared
dash of pepper
¼ tsp. Tabasco sauce
1¼ tbls. lemon juice

Blend ingredients, in the order given, and mix well. A perfect all-around dressing for vegetable, meat or fish salad.

267. Cream Dressing (*Rahmmarinade*)

1 tsp. mustard, prepared
1 tsp. salt
1½ tsp. confectioner's sugar
dash of pepper
2 tbls. flour
1 tsp. butter
1 egg yolk
⅓ cup vinegar
¼ cup heavy cream, whipped

In double boiler, over hot, not boiling, water, beat mustard, salt, sugar, pepper, flour and butter. Add egg yolk and vinegar and continue beating until mixture thickens. Remove from heat. When cool, fold in whipped cream. This dressing may be served with any vegetable, meat or green salad.

SAUCES, ASPIC AND BUTTERS
(*Saucen, Aspik und Buttersorten*)

268. Butter Sauce (*Buttersauce*)

3 tbls. flour
4 tbls. butter
2 cups water
salt and pepper
2 egg yolks, beaten, or
    ¼ cup cream

Brown flour in butter over medium heat. Add water gradually, stirring constantly to form a smooth sauce. Season and continue stirring until sauce thickens. The sauce may be enriched by adding egg yolks or cream which should be well blended.

269. Béchamel Sauce (*Béchamelsauce*)

1¼ cups Butter Sauce
    (No. 268)
½ cup cream
4 tbls. cheese, grated

Prepare Butter Sauce. Add cream and grated cheese and let cook briefly together to blend thoroughly.

270. Brown Sauce *(Braune Sauce)*

3 tbls. butter
4 tbls. flour
1 onion, chopped
2 cups water
1 bay leaf
2 cloves
2 tbls. vinegar
salt and pepper
paprika

Melt butter, add flour and slowly brown. Mix in onion. Add water little by little, stirring constantly. Season. Bring to a boil. Strain before serving.

271. Madeira Sauce *(Madeirasauce)*

1½ cups Brown Sauce
(No. 270)
¼ cup Madeira wine

Prepare Brown Sauce. Just before serving add and stir in Madeira, but do not cook further.

272. Hollandaise Sauce *(Holländische Sauce)*

2 egg yolks
1 tbls. lemon juice
1 tbls. water
salt and pepper
nutmeg
pinch of sugar
7 tbls. butter

Mix all ingredients, except butter, in top of double boiler. Do not let water in bottom boil. Beat well, over moderate heat. Add butter, by spoonfuls, and keep beating until sauce is rich and thick.

273. Sauce Bernaise *(Berner Sauce)*

4 tbls. white wine
3 tbls. wine vinegar
1 clove
3 shallots
1 small stem tarragon
½ bay leaf
salt
peppercorns
2 egg yolks
10 tbls. butter

Bring wine, vinegar and spices to a boil. Strain. When cool, stir in egg yolks and half the butter. Place in double boiler, over hot, *not boiling*, water and gradually add remaining butter, beating constantly until thick.

274. Mousseline Sauce (*Mousselinsauce*)

2 egg yolks
1 tbls. flour
1 tbls. butter
salt and pepper
lemon juice
1 cup heavy cream, whipped

Beat egg yolks, flour, butter and seasoning to a heavy froth in top of double boiler over hot, not boiling, water. Just before serving add lemon juice to taste and fold in whipped cream.

275. Hot Mayonnaise (*Heisse Mayonnaise*)

2 egg yolks
1½ tsp. flour
2 tbls. olive oil
1 tbls. vinegar
¼ cup hot water
salt and pepper
1 tsp. parsley, chopped

Blend egg yolks and flour. Add, little by little, olive oil, vinegar and water, stirring constantly. Cook in top of double boiler over hot, not boiling, water, still stirring until mixture thickens. Season and sprinkle with chopped parsley.

276. Russian Sauce (*Russische Sauce*)

3 tbls. butter
2 tbls. flour
1 cup beef stock
salt
peppercorns
½ tsp. chives, chopped
¼ tsp. mustard, prepared
1 tbls. horseradish
¼ cup cream
1 tsp. lemon juice

Melt butter, add flour, blend and gradually add the beef stock. Stir in seasoning, chives, mustard and horseradish. Cook for 2 minutes. Strain. Add cream and lemon juice and bring to a boil.

277. Orange Sauce (*Orangensauce*)

¼ cup butter
¼ cup flour
½ tsp. salt
dash cayenne pepper
1⅓ cups beef stock
juice of 2 oranges
2 tbls. sherry
peel of 1 orange, grated

Brown the butter, add flour, salt and cayenne pepper. Mix well and add, little by little, the beef stock. Just before serving, add orange juice, sherry and orange peel.

278. Spanish Sauce (*Spanische Sauce*)

1½ cups Brown Sauce (No. 270)
1 bouillon cube
1 tbls. lemon juice
1½ tbls. parsley, chopped fine
1 tbls. butter
salt and pepper

Prepare Brown Sauce. Dissolve bouillon cube in 2 tablespoons boiling water, and add, together with lemon juice and parsley. Just before serving, add butter and season to taste. This is sometimes called Parsley Sauce.

279. Remoulade Sauce (*Remouladensauce*)

½ cup mayonnaise
1 tsp. mustard
1 tsp. salad herbs, chopped
1 tsp. capers
1 small pickle, chopped
cream

Blend the first five ingredients and then thin with cream to desired consistency.

280. Tartar Sauce (*Tartarsauce*)

1 tbls. vinegar
1 tsp. lemon juice
¼ tsp. salt
1 tbls. Worcestershire Sauce
⅓ cup butter

Mix vinegar, lemon juice, salt and Worcestershire sauce in small bowl. Heat in top of double boiler. Brown butter and fold into sauce just before serving.

281. Horseradish Sauce (*Meerrettichsauce*)

2 tbls. butter
2 tbls. flour
1 cup milk
1 small onion, chopped
a few almonds, chopped
1 tsp. sugar
pinch of salt and pepper
2 tbls. horseradish

Melt butter but do not brown. Add flour and gradually stir in milk. Add chopped onion, almonds, sugar, salt and pepper. Cook together for 15 minutes, over low heat or in double boiler. Before serving, fold in horseradish and, if desired, enrich with a little butter or cream.

282. Mustard or Caper Sauce
(Senf-oder Kapernsauce)

1½ cups Butter Sauce
   (No. 268)
1 small onion, chopped
1 tbls. vinegar
sugar
salt and pepper
4 tbls. prepared mustard, or
   capers

Prepare Butter Sauce and to it add onion, vinegar and seasoning. Fold in mustard or capers and bring to a boil.

283. Onion Sauce (Zwiebelsauce)

1 large onion
2 tbls. butter
3 tbls. flour
2 cups beef stock
1 tbls. vinegar
Maggi
salt and pepper
2 tbls. dry white wine
½ tsp. lemon juice

Slice onion thinly and sauté in butter until golden. Sprinkle in flour and brown. Gradually add beef stock, vinegar and seasoning and bring to a boil. Before serving, strain and season with wine and lemon juice.

284. Tomato Sauce (Tomatensauce)

1 lb. tomatoes
2 cups water
pinch of salt
3 tbls. butter
3 tbls. flour
1 tsp. sugar
1 tsp. paprika
3 tbls. milk, if needed

Quarter the tomatoes and cook in slightly salted water until soft. Prepare a light roux from butter and flour, thinned with water. Put tomatoes through a sieve and add to roux. Season well. Bring to a boil. If sauce is too thick, thin with a few spoonfuls of milk.

285. Cucumber Sauce *(Gurkensauce)*

2 cups Butter Sauce
   (No. 268)
1 tbls. vinegar
salt and pepper
sugar
10 small cucumber pickles
1-2 tbls. cream

Prepare Butter Sauce. Add vinegar and seasonings to taste and bring to a boil. Slice cucumber pickles, add to sauce and heat briefly. Just before serving add cream.

286. Danish Fish Sauce *(Dänische Fischsauce)*

2 tbls. butter
3 tbls. flour
2 cups water, hot
2 egg yolks, beaten
salt and pepper
Anchovy Butter (No. 301)
   to taste

Cream butter. Add flour and hot water and stir well, over low heat, until sauce begins to boil. Remove from heat. Stir in egg yolks and season well. Before serving blend in a little Anchovy Butter. Goes with all kinds of fish.

287. Dutch Parsley Sauce
(Holländische Petersiliensauce)

1 large bunch parsley
   (German says "handful")
1½ cups Butter Sauce
   (No. 268)
1 egg yolk
2 tbls. cream
salt
lemon juice to taste
1 tbls. butter

Remove stems of parsley and cook leaves in water for 5 minutes. Prepare Butter Sauce and add to parsley and water. Over low heat, add egg yolk, cream, salt and lemon juice. Stir well and, finally, add butter and blend to a smooth sauce.

288. Cumberland Sauce *(Cumberlandsauce)*

peel of ½ orange
3 tbls. currant jelly.
2 tsp. prepared mustard
2 tbls. olive oil
dash of salt
1 tbls. lemon juice

Remove white inner layer from orange peel. Chop peel finely and scald. Melt currant jelly over low heat. Add mustard and all other ingredients and stir sauce to a smooth texture. Popular with venison and other game, and with cold fish.

289. Sauce Vinaigrette

2 hard-cooked eggs, chopped
a few cucumber pickles,
    chopped
1 tbls. parsley, chopped
1 small onion, chopped
2 tbls. vinegar
4 tbls. olive oil
mustard, sugar, salt, pepper,
    to taste

Mix all chopped ingredients thoroughly with vinegar, oil and seasonings. If sauce is too sharp, dilute with a few teaspoonfuls of water.

290. Sauce Ravigote *(Ravigotesauce)*

2 tbls. prepared mustard
2 tbls. vinegar
2 tbls. olive oil
salt and pepper to taste
2 tbls. parsley, chopped
1 tbls. chervil, dried
2 yolks of hard-cooked eggs,
    chopped

Mix mustard, vinegar, oil, salt and pepper. Stir in chopped parsley, chervil and egg yolks.

291. Mayonnaise

1 egg yolk, raw
lemon juice
pinch of flour
salt
prepared mustard
1 cup olive oil
pinch of sugar
½ tbls. vinegar

Beat egg yolk and stir in a few drops of lemon juice, flour, salt and mustard. In the beginning add oil carefully and in very small quantities (drop by drop) to keep mayonnaise from thickening too rapidly. Toward the end, less care is necessary in adding oil. Thin thick mayonnaise with lemon juice and oil. Season with sugar and vinegar and chill before serving.

292. Fool-Proof Mayonnaise
(Mayonnaise, auf ganz sicher)

3 egg yolks
4 tbls. olive oil
3 tbls. beef stock
1 tbls. vinegar
pinch of salt, pinch of
   pepper, pinch of sugar
lemon juice and mustard,
   to taste

Mix all ingredients in top of double-boiler and beat to a froth. When well-blended, remove from heat and stir while mayonnaise cools. Chill before serving.

293. Aspic (Aspik)

2 cups white wine
2 cups water
Maggi
pinch of salt
4 tbls. vinegar
2½ envelopes gelatine
   in ½ cup water

Bring wine, water, Maggi, salt and vinegar to a boil. Dissolve gelatine in ½ cup water and mix with liquid. Turn out in large, shallow pan and cool. Cut into cubes.

Aspic is a fine garnish for cold meat platters, patties and salads. Aspic may also be used to prepare jellied meat: Fill individual molds (or one large mold) ½ inch deep with liquid aspic. Chill. On this put cold cuts, sliced hard-cooked eggs, pickles, tomatoes, cooked peas, beans or any desired filling. Then fill mold with liquid aspic and chill. Dip dishes in hot water and loosen edges of aspic with a knife to turn out easily.

294. Melted Butter (Zerlassene Butter)

¼ lb. butter

Melt butter in a small pan over moderate heat until there is no solid left, but do not lose its golden yellow color.

295. Brown Butter *(Braune Butter)*

¼ lb. butter

Melt butter in small pan over moderate, heat, as above, but allow it to turn *light* brown.

296. Onion Butter *(Zwiebelbutter)*

4 tbls. butter
1 onion

Chop onion finely and sauté in butter until golden.

297. Truffle Butter *(Trüffelbutter)*

5 tbls. butter
2 truffles
1 tsp. Madeira wine
salt and pepper

Cream the butter. Chop truffles finely, add wine and seasoning and mix well with butter.

298. Major-Domo Butter *(Haushofmeisterbutter)*

3 tbls. butter
2 tsp. parsley, chopped
juice of ½ lemon
salt and pepper
Worcestershire sauce

Cream butter well, mix parsley, lemon juice and seasoning. Just before serving add a few drops of Worcestershire sauce. Popular with meat or fish.

299. Herb Butter *(Krauterbutter)*

2 cups assorted herbs,
    chopped
2 leaves of spinach
1 shallot
1 bud garlic
juice of ½ lemon
salt
7 tbls. butter

Boil herbs briefly, drain, dry in towel and chop finely. Chop spinach leaves and shallots with garlic, lemon juice, salt and herbs. Put all through a strainer. Cream butter and add.

300. Mustard Butter *(Senfbutter)*

1 hard-cooked egg yolk
4 tbls. butter
1 tbls. prepared mustard
1 tbls. lemon juice
salt and pepper

Press egg yolk through strainer and mix well with all other ingredients.

301. Anchovy Butter *(Sardellenbutter)*

6 anchovies
5 tbls. butter

Bone and chop anchovies finely. Pass through strainer. Cream butter and blend with anchovies.

302. Salmon Butter *(Lachsbutter)*

5 tbls. butter
¼ cup smoked salmon, boned

Cream butter, chop salmon very fine and mix well.

303. Smoked Herring Butter *(Bücklingbutter)*

5 tbls. butter
1 smoked herring fillet
pepper

Cream butter. Mash herring fillet with fork and blend with butter. Season with pepper.

304. Flour Butter *(Mehlbutter)*

4 tsp. butter
3 tsp. flour

Knead butter and flour and tuck into hot, freshly cooked vegetables. Do not cook, or taste of flour will be too noticeable.

LUNCHEON DISHES AND OTHER SPECIALTIES

(Spezialitäten, Eintopfgerichte und Zwischengerichte)

305. Ragout in Shells *(Ragout fin in Muscheln)*

1 small ox tongue
1 onion
1 bay leaf
salt
1 sweetbread
1 cup mushrooms
4-5 tbls. butter
3 anchovies
2 tbls. flour
¼ cup white wine
1 egg yolk
lemon juice
Patty Shells (No. 307)
1 cup grated cheese
extra butter
lemon slices and parsley

Cook ox tongue with seasonings for about an hour, or until skin peels off easily. Save water. Skin and dice. Blanch sweetbreads. Add mushrooms and butter and stew for 10 minutes. Chop finely. Chop anchovies and mix them and the diced tongue with the sweetbreads and mushrooms. Stir flour into wine, add one cup of cooking water. Blend with ragout and cook all ingredients together briefly. Season to taste and add some lemon juice; thicken with egg yolk. Turn out into shells. Sprinkle with grated cheese, butter and more lemon juice and bake in a hot (425°) oven until cheese is brown, 5 to 10 minutes. Garnish platter with lemon slices and parsley.
Serves 4.

306. Poultry Pie (Geflügelpastete)

1¼ lbs. poultry meat
2 tbls. flour
1 tbls. butter
1 cup water
4 eggs, separated
1 cup sweet cream
salt and pepper
1 tbls. butter
1 large onion
½ cup grated cheese
truffles

Grind meat of chicken, goose, turkey, duck, pheasant, partridge or any combination of same. Brown flour in butter, add water and cook to firm consistency. Strain, mix into meat, add egg yolks, cream and seasoning. Lightly brown in butter finely chopped onion and mix this, together with grated cheese and beaten egg whites, with previous mixture. Put in well-greased pie dish, put minced truffles on top and bake in a hot (425°) oven for 40 minutes. May be served hot or cold. Serve with Hollandaise Sauce (No. 272).

Serves 6.

307. Patty Shells (Pastetchen)

Laminated Dough
(No. 451)

Prepare dough in 4 to 6 "courses." Roll out 1/6 inch thick. Cut out 2-inch rounds, preferably with a wavy-edged cutter. Place half of these, upside down, on a wet or greased baking sheet. Form rings of the other half, by cutting out centers. Brush underside of rings with egg white, being careful egg white does not run over edges, as dough will not rise properly in such spots. The little round centers of the ring can be used to top the filling. Brush patty and cover with egg yolk and bake in hot (400°) oven for 25 minutes, until golden brown Fill while still hot and serve.

Makes 12-14.

308. Royal Patties *(Königinpastetchen)*

Patty Shells (No. 307)
2 cups cooked chicken,
　　chopped fine
¾ cup cooked tongue,
　　chopped fine
6 mushrooms, chopped fine
2 tbls. butter
1 tbls. flour
½ cup beef or soup stock
salt and pepper
1 tsp. lemon juice
4 tbls. wine
1 egg yolk

Prepare shells. Sauté chopped chicken, tongue and mushrooms briefly in butter. Sprinkle with flour and, gradually, add beef or soup stock. Add seasoning, lemon juice and wine to taste. Thicken with egg yolk. Fill patties while still hot and serve immediately.

309. Chicken Patties *(Hühnerpastete)*

1 lb. chicken meat
2 tbls. flour
1 tbls. butter
1 cup water
4 eggs, separated
1 cup cream
salt and pepper
1 big onion
1 tbls. butter
4 tbls. grated cheese
1 truffle, chopped

Bone cooked chicken and put through meat grinder. Brown flour lightly in butter, add water. Cook and stir until thickened. Cool and put through a strainer, then blend with the meat, egg yolk, cream and seasoning. Chop onion, lightly brown in butter and add to the mixture. Sprinkle with grated cheese. Beat egg whites and fold in. Grease well individual baking dishes, put a piece of truffle in each and fill. Bake in a hot (425°) oven for about 40 minutes. Serve hot or cold. If served cold, serve with Remoulade Sauce (No. 279).

Serves 6.

310. Ham Pie *(Schinkenpastete)*

Laminated Dough (No. 451)
(using 1¼ cups flour)

Filling:
½ lb. pork, cooked
½ lb. veal, cooked
1 roll
1 onion
parsley
2 eggs, separated
pinch of basil
2 tbls. fat
2 tsp. Madeira wine

4 slices ham (measuring
2½ x 5 inches)

Prepare dough. Roll out one-half of the dough in a rectangle 6 by 11 inches. Fill as follows:
Grind meat. Soak roll in water and squeeze dry. Pluck apart. Chop onion and parsley. Add egg yolks (saving 1 tablespoon) and seasoning. Beat whites of eggs until stiff (saving 1 tablespoon) and fold in. Combine all ingredients (except ham). Place slices of ham on dough to within ½ inch of edges. Cover with mixture, then with other ham slices. Spread egg white on edges of dough. Roll out remaining dough and place it over all, pressing edges firmly together. Trim overlapping dough and from it form ¾-inch strips to place criss-cross on top of pie. Brush with egg yolk and bake in a medium (375°) oven about 1 hour. Serve hot or cold.
Serves 6.

311. Cheese Delights *(Käsepastetchen)*

5 tbls. butter
4 eggs
1 cup sour cream
½ cup grated cheese
1 tbls. flour
salt and paprika

Cream butter. Separate eggs. Add egg yolks, sour cream, grated cheese, flour and salt and paprika. Mix well. Beat egg whites until stiff and fold in. Grease oven-proof custard cups and fill with mixture. Bake in hot (425°) oven 20 to 25 minutes. Serve hot.
Serves 4.

312. Potato Patties *(Kartoffelpastetchen)*

4-5 medium potatoes
½ cup milk
1-2 tbls. butter
salt and nutmeg

Filling:
1 roll
2 tbls. milk
1 onion
1 tbls. parsley
1 tbls. butter
½ cup chopped roast veal
3 tbls. gravy of veal roast
1 egg, separated
salt, pepper and nutmeg

Boil and mash potatoes. Mix with milk, butter, and seasonings to make a thick batter (potato purée). Butter a baking sheet. Make 8 little round cakes from dough. With cake decorator form rims around edges and bake until light brown. Make filling as follows:
Soak roll in milk, squeeze dry, break up. Chop onion and parsley and cook in butter. Add veal, gravy, beaten yolk, beaten white and seasoning. Put in patties and bake in a medium (375°) oven until well browned.
Serves 4.

313. Rissole of Brain *(Rissolen mit Gehirn)*

5-6 tbls. butter
2 cups flour
1 egg
salt
fat for frying

Filling:

1 lb. calf's brain
4 tbls. butter
2 tbls. flour
1 egg yolk
½ cup white wine
lemon juice
salt
4 mushrooms

Cream butter, add flour, eggs (save a little egg white for moistening) and salt. Mix thoroughly into a pliable dough and roll about 1/12 inch thick on a floured board. Cut with round cutter. On each circular piece put a walnut-sized heap of filling (see below).
Moisten edge with egg white, cover with another circular piece and press sides firmly together. Cook in deep fat until golden-yellow.

Filling:
Blanch the brains (place in cold water, scald), skin and chop fine. Melt butter, brown flour, add egg yolk, wine, lemon juice and seasoning to taste. Chop mushrooms and add. Cook briefly and let cool.
Serves 4.

314. Chicken Croquettes, Macedon
(*Mazedonische Hühnercroquetten*)

1 small onion
3 tbls. butter
¼ cup flour
salt, pepper and paprika
1 cup chicken gravy
1 cup cooked chicken, diced
3 egg yolks
½ cup chopped mushrooms
2 eggs
flour and bread crumbs
fat

Chop onion and brown in butter. Add flour and seasoning. Blend well and stir in gravy. Bring to a boil and add chicken, egg yolks and mushrooms. Cook 5 minutes. Cool. Turn out onto a plate and form into small elliptical cakes. Mix eggs, flour and crumbs. Dip cakes in this mixture. Fry in deep fat and let drain on a paper. Serve on a hot flat platter. Surround with peas, carrots and cauliflower rosettes. Garnish with parsley.

Serves 4-6.

315. Chicken Timbales

2 tbls. butter
¼ cup bread crumbs
⅔ cup milk
1 cup cooked, chopped
   chicken
½ tbls. minced parsley
2 eggs
salt and pepper

Melt butter, add crumbs and milk. Cook for 5 minutes, stirring continuously. Add chopped chicken, parsley, lightly beaten eggs and seasonings. Grease individual custard (pyrex) cups and fill. Place in a hot water pan (filled to two-thirds height of dishes). Cover each cup with wax paper and bake for 20 minutes in 350° oven.

Serves 4-6.

316. Salmon Soufflé

1 tall 17-ounce can salmon
½ cup bread crumbs
¼ cup milk
3 eggs, separated
2 tsp. lemon juice
salt and paprika

Flake canned salmon. Cook bread crumbs in milk for 5 minutes. Beat egg yolks, add lemon juice, fish and seasoning. Beat egg whites and fold in. Grease baking dish and pour in mixture. Place in water pan and cook in oven at moderate (350°) heat until quite firm, about 30 minutes. Serve with Spanish Sauce (No. 278) or Dutch Parsley Sauce (No. 287).
Serves 4-6.

317. Stuffed Eggs (Gefüllte Eier)

4 hard-cooked eggs
2 very thin slices ham
1 anchovy
½ small onion
1 knife-point mustard
1 tsp. vinegar
1 tsp. oil
salt and pepper

Slice eggs in half lengthwise. Remove yolks and press through strainer. Chop finely ham, anchovy, onion. Add seasoning. Mix well with yolks. Stuff egg whites. Any excess stuffing may be used to decorate platter. Sprinkle eggs lightly with flour, dot with butter and heat gently in moderate (350°) oven for 15 minutes before serving.
Serves 4.

318. Creamed Tomatoes (Tomaten à la Crème)

6 tomatoes
salt and pepper
2 tbls. flour
2 tbls. butter

Scald, peel and slice tomatoes thickly. Season well. Sprinkle with flour and fry in butter. Serve on a hot platter, covered with Butter Sauce (No. 268).
Serves 4-6.

319.   Devil's Tomatoes *(Teufelstomaten)*

3 tomatoes
salt and pepper
½ tbls. flour
butter for frying
5 tbls. butter
1 cooked egg yolk
1 whole egg
2 tsp. powdered sugar
¼ tsp. salt
1 tsp. mustard
2 tbls. vinegar

Scald, peel and slice tomatoes. Season well. Sprinkle with flour and fry in butter. Keep hot while making sauce, as follows:
Cream butter, mash yolk, beat and add whole egg. Mix in other ingredients. Cook in double boiler, stirring continuously until sauce thickens. Pour over tomatoes and serve.
Serves 2.

320.   Mushroom Entrée *(Pilze im Glas)*

2 tbls. butter
½ tbls. lemon juice
salt and pepper
¼ tsp. finely chopped parsley
white bread
½ lb. mushrooms
¼ cup cream
1 tsp. sherry

Cream butter. Add lemon juice drop by drop, salt, pepper and parsley. Cut two ½ inch thick rounds of bread and toast. Spread with butter mixture on both sides and put in individual buttered (greased) baking dishes. Clean and peel mushrooms. Heap on toasted sections and pour cream over. Bake, covered, in 350° oven for 25 minutes, adding additional cream if desired. Just before serving, add sherry.
Serves 2.

321.   Fondue Neuchâtel *(Fondue, Neuchâteler Art)*

garlic
4 whole eggs
salt and pepper
1 cup dry white wine
½ lb. Swiss cheese, cubed
4 tbls. butter
2 jigger cherry brandy
cubes of toast, optional

Rub flameproof dish with garlic. Break in eggs, beat lightly, add seasoning and wine. Add cheese and flakes of butter and stir, over moderate heat, until mixture is thick. Pour on cherry brandy. Cubes of toast may be dropped in fondue. This should be cooked in the dish in which it will be served.
Serves 4.

322. Bernaise Sandwich (*Berner Brötchen*)

1 tbls. butter
1 tbls. flour
⅓ cup cream
4 slices cooked ham
toast
2 tbls. Swiss cheese, grated

Melt butter, stir in flour smoothly. Blend in cream, stirring until thickened. Chop ham and add to sauce. Heap on toast. Top with Swiss cheese and broil lightly. Serves 2.

323. Snails (*Schnecken*)

3 dozen snails
1 tsp. salt
1 cup beef stock
1 cup Burgundy
seasoning, to taste
Herb Butter (No. 299)

Wash snails and cook in boiling salted water until the covers come off easily. With a needle, lift snails out of shells and remove all dark spots, including head, cartilage and tail ends. Cook snails until tender in beef stock, Burgundy and seasoning. Brush shells clean and drop into boiling water with a pinch of baking soda. Rinse shells and put snails back in them. Top each one with Herb Butter. Arrange in a pan, with openings up. If you have difficulty keeping snails upright, put a layer of salt in the pan and press shells into it. Bake in a hot (375°) oven until butter begins to bubble, just a few minutes. Or put briefly under the broiler. Serves 3-6.

324. Dried Peas, The Berlin Way
(Löffelerbsen nach Berliner Art)

1 lb. dried peas
1 onion
1 leak
1 small celery knob
1 tbls. butter
1 lb. pig's ear and snout
thyme or marjoram
salt and pepper
2 potatoes, raw, chopped fine

Soak peas overnight. Dice other vegetables and sauté lightly in butter in a fairly large pan. Add peas and fill up with water. Cook one hour, add meat, cubed, and seasoning and continue cooking until tender, 2 to 3 hours in all. To bind, add raw potatoes 20 minutes before serving.
Serves 4.

325. Cabbage Rolls (Krautwickel)

1 head cabbage
1 lb. mixed ground meat
    (beef and pork)
1 egg
1 onion, chopped
1 tsp. parsley, chopped
1 tsp. butter
1 cup beef stock
1 tbls. flour
4 tbls. cream

Remove large outer leaves of cabbage, flatten out ribs and cook in salted water 2 to 3 minutes. Drain and spread out on table. Chop small leaves finely and mix with meat, egg, onion and parsley for stuffing. Spread stuffing on large leaves, roll up and tie. Fry rolls briefly in butter, pour on beef stock, cover and let simmer over low heat for 1 hour. Or simmer for ¾ hour and bake in moderate (350°) oven for 15 minutes. Place on hot platter. Add flour and cream to pan to prepare gravy. Pour over rolls to serve. Serve with Salted Potatoes (No. 199).
Serves 4.

326. Stuffed Peppers (Gefüllter Paprika)

4 large peppers
1 cup ground meat, mixed
   beef and pork
1 cup rice, cooked
1 egg
salt and pepper
paprika
1 tsp. parsley, chopped
3 tbls. butter
water
2 cups Tomato Sauce
   (No. 284)

Remove stems (if any) of peppers, cut off the bottoms and save them. Scoop out seeds. Mix meat with rice and egg and season well. Add parsley. Stuff this mixture in peppers and replace bottoms. Place peppers upright in a casserole. Add butter and a little water, cover and stew over moderate heat until done. Pour thick Tomato Sauce over peppers, heat thoroughly and serve.
Serves 4.

327. Stuffed Cabbage (Gefüllter Krautkopf)

1 head cabbage
1½ lbs. ground meat, mixed
   beef and pork
1 roll, soaked, squeezed dry
   and broken up
1 tsp. parsley, chopped
1 onion, chopped
1 egg
salt and pepper

Break off leaves of cabbage, flatten thick ribs, and cook in salted water 2 to 3 minutes. Drain and spread out to cool. Mix meat, roll, parsley, onion, egg and seasoning. Moisten with water. Dip a napkin in hot water and spread it out in a medium-sized bowl. Place cabbage leaves on napkin so that tips of leaves overlap in the center. Alternate layers of stuffing and leaves. Lift the four corners of the napkin and tie in a sling. Place a wooden kitchen spoon across the top of cooking pot and suspend sling from this so napkin will be nearly submerged in cooking water. Simmer for about 1½ hours. Untie napkin and turn stuffed cabbage out on a hot platter. Serve with Salted Potatoes (No. 199), Melted Butter (No. 294) or Tomato Sauce (No. 284).
Serves 4.

328. Liver Spätzle (Leberspätzle)

¾ lb. beef liver
4 cups flour
2 eggs
1 tbls. salt
water
Onion Butter (No. 296)

Grind liver. Mix with flour, eggs, salt and enough water to form a smooth dough. Beat until mixture comes away from the sides of the bowl easily. Form small batches of dough into dumplings and drop into lightly salted boiling water. Dip out and serve on a hot platter, topped with Onion Butter. Serve with Potato Salad (No. 258) or a green salad. Serves 4.

329. Liver Patties (Leberklosse, feine)

1 onion, chopped
2 tbls. parsley, chopped
1 tsp. marjoram
salt and pepper
1 tsp. butter
4 eggs
1 lb. calf's liver, finely
    chopped
1 cup (about) half flour,
    half cornmeal
beef stock

Brown the onion, parsley and seasonings in butter. While still warm, add eggs and stir. Mix in the liver and enough of the flour-cornmeal mixture to form patties. Bring beef stock to a boil. Place patties in this and cook until they rise to the surface. Serve with Onion Butter (No. 296).
Serves 4.

330. Konigsberger Meat Balls
(*Königsberger Klopse*)

1 roll
1 lb. ground meat, mixed
    beef and pork
3 potatoes, cooked and
    mashed
2 anchovies, chopped
1 egg
flour, to bind
3 tbls. butter
2 tbls. flour
1 cup beef stock
capers
juice of ½ lemon
salt and pepper

Soak roll in water, squeeze dry and break up. Add meat, potatoes, anchovies, egg and flour to bind. Knead mixture for 5 minutes and shape into balls. Tumble in flour and drop into salted hot water. Simmer for 12 to 15 minutes. From butter, flour and beef stock, prepare a light sauce. When smooth add capers and lemon juice. Season and bring to a boil. Let meat balls soak briefly in this before serving. Serve with Salted Potatoes (No. 199).
Serves 4.

331. Pichelsteiner Stew (*Pichelsteiner*)

1 lb. meat, mixed (beef,
    pork, lamb)
1 small head cabbage
½ lb. turnips
¼ lb. string beans
1 celery knob
½ lb. potatoes
1 onion
1 tsp. parsley, chopped
salt and pepper
paprika
¼ lb. beef marrow,
    sliced thin
butter
2 cups beef stock

Cut up meat and vegetables in fairly large chunks. Keep separate. Season well. Select a cooking pot with a tight-fitting lid. Cover bottom of pot with marrow, and on this alternate layers of meat and vegetables. Top with marrow and dot with butter. Add beef stock, cover and stew over low heat for 2 hours, or until meat is tender. Tilt or shake the pan occasionally to keep stew from sticking to bottom and burning.
Serves 4.

332. Hungarian Goulash
(Ungarischer Gulasch-Eintopf)

2 lbs. stew beef
¼ lb. pork fat
1 lb. onions, chopped fine
salt
2 tbls. paprika
1½ lbs. potatoes

Cut up meat in rather large cubes. Melt fat in large pot and sauté onions. Salt the meat and add, letting it fry until fat is absorbed. Sprinkle generously with paprika. Pour on water to cover, cover and stew 1½ hours. Peel potatoes, cut into thin wedges, add to stew, cook ½ hour longer or until meat is tender. Add more water if necessary.

Serves 6.

333. Lamb Stew (Hammelfleisch-Eintopf)

3 lbs. breast of lamb
soup greens
salt
2 lbs. potatoes
caraway seeds
vinegar to taste
pepper
2 strips bacon
1 tbls. flour

Cook lamb and soup greens in salted water about 1 hour. When done, remove meat from bones and cut up. Strain cooking water and replace in pot. Cut potatoes in fairly thick slices and add to liquid. Season well with caraway seeds, vinegar and pepper and cook until potatoes are done. Meanwhile fry bacon lightly in skillet. Sprinkle in flour, add a cup of the liquid, blend and add to potatoes. Finally replace meat in stew and cook everything together briefly.

Serves 4.

334. Schnitzel Stew *(Schnitzel-Eintopf)*

1¼ lbs. bottom round
1 large onion, chopped
4 tbls. butter
1 medium bunch carrots,
    sliced
4 medium potatoes, sliced
1½ cups beef stock
salt and pepper
½ cup cream
1 tbls. ketchup
1 tbls. flour
parsley

Have meat cut in 4 pieces ½ inch thick. Brown meat and onion lightly in butter. Add carrots and potatoes. Pour on beef stock, season, cover, and simmer until done, about 30 minutes. Blend cream, ketchup and flour. Add to stew and bring briefly to a boil. Garnish with parsley to serve.

Serves 4.

335. Meat and Bean Stew *(Bohnen-Eintopf)*

1 lb. beef or pork
1 small onion
1 bud garlic
pinch of ginger
salt and pepper
3 tbls. butter
1 lb. green beans, sliced
1 lb. potatoes, wedged

Cube meat and onion. Season and fry lightly together in butter. Add water to cover and cook for 30 minutes over moderate heat. Add beans and potatoes and continue cooking until done, about 20 minutes more.

Serves 4.

336. Hunter's Stew *(Jäger-Eintopf)*

6 tbls. butter
1 lb. beef, cubed
½ lb. onions
1 lb. mushrooms, sliced
beef stock, as needed
salt and pepper
1 tbls. parsley, chopped
4 medium potatoes
1 tbls. flour

Melt butter and in it lightly fry meat and onions. Add mushrooms, beef stock and seasonings and stew for about 1½ hours. Turn frequently and add extra beef stock as needed. Cut potatoes in wedges and add. Continue to add beef stock, or water, as needed. When potatoes are done, thicken gravy with flour.

Serves 4.

337. Turnip Stew (*Rüben-Eintopf*)

1½ lbs. small turnips
2 lbs. breast of lamb
salt, paprika, ginger
2 tbls. butter, to braise
2 tomatoes, halved
4 tbls. flour
2 tbls. butter, for sauce
2 cups beef stock

Cook turnips 15 minutes in lightly salted water. Rub lamb generously with seasonings and braise in butter with tomatoes. Drain and add turnips. Prepare a sauce from flour, butter and beef stock, seasoned to taste. Pour this over stew, cover, and simmer over slow heat for another hour.
Serves 4.

338. Silesian Heaven (*Birnen-Eintopf*)

1 lb. smoked ham, cubed
1½ lbs. Seckel pears
salt and pepper
1 lb. small new potatoes

Barely cover bottom of baking dish with water. Season meat and place in center of dish. Remove stems from pears but do not pare. Place pears around meat. Peel potatoes, salt them, and place these, too, around meat. Cover and bake in moderate (350°) oven, adding warm water as needed, until all ingredients are tender, about 1 hour. Do not overcook or pears and potatoes will fall apart.
Serves 4.

339. Winter Stew (*Winter-Eintopf*)

1 lb. chestnuts
½ lb. yellow turnips
¾ lb. leeks
2 tbls. butter
salt and pepper
4 large sausages

Shell chestnuts. Clean and dice turnips and leeks. Melt butter in pot, add chestnuts and vegetables. Cover with water, season and stew until done, about 30 minutes. Fry sausages. Place on vegetables. Pour cooking fat over this to serve.
Serves 4.

340. Cabbage with Bacon (*Weisskraut mit Speck*)

2 lbs. cabbage
1½ lbs. potatoes
salt, paprika, caraway seeds
½ lb. bacon
1 onion

Cut cabbage in strips and cook for 10 minutes in salted water. Peel and dice potatoes and add to cabbage. Season. Cook until potatoes are done, about 20 minutes. Drain cabbage. Chop up bacon and onion and brown together and combine with cabbage and potatoes.
Serves 4.

341. Baked Asparagus (*Spargelgericht, überbacken*)

1½ lbs. asparagus, cooked
2 lbs. potatoes, cooked
    and sliced
½ lb. ham, thinly sliced
1 tbls. parsley, chopped
4 tbls. cheese, grated
2 cups Butter Sauce
    (No. 268)
salt, nutmeg, pepper
1 egg yolk
2 tbls. butter

In a well-greased baking dish, place alternate layers of asparagus (halved), potatoes, and ham. Sprinkle with parsley and half the cheese. Prepare Butter Sauce, using asparagus water as liquid. Season well and stir in egg yolk. Blend and pour over casserole. Sprinkle with remaining cheese, dot with butter and brown in moderate (375°) oven.
Serves 4.

342. Pancakes (*Pfannkuchen*)

4 cups flour
3-4 eggs
salt
3 cups milk
fat

Pancakes should be prepared about an hour in advance. Pour flour into bowl, make a depression in the center into which put eggs, some salt and lukewarm milk (or half water and half milk). Stir until well blended. If thin pancakes (*fladle*) are desired, batter should be thin; for heartier cakes, batter should be thicker. This can be controlled by adding more or less liquid. Drop a little batter on a greased skillet; let it spread out, and fry to a golden brown on both sides. Serve immediately, or keep warm on a hot platter, preferably in the oven.

There are countless variations to serving pancakes: sprinkled with lemon juice and sugar; as an accompaniment to stewed fruits, berries, or salads; with jelly, marmalade, Vanilla Cream (No. 413) or Chocolate Cream (No. 414). Thin pancakes may be filled with spinach, mushrooms, chopped ham, beef or sausages and rolled up. Or they may be rolled, cut in finger-length pieces, sprinkled with grated cheese, dotted with butter and baked briefly in a moderate oven. The batter itself may be varied by the addition of intriguing ingredients such as cubed ham, crumbled bacon, cubed Swiss cheese, spicy herbs or chopped fruits. These variations are then prepared in the usual manner.

Serves 4-6.

343. Puff-Pie Crust *(Pastenteig)*

¼ lb. suet fat or butter
2 cups flour
1 egg
2 tbls. water
pinch of salt

Melt suet and work into all other ingredi٦
ents to make a smooth firm dough. Roll
out and use as instructed in specific
recipe.

344. Sauerkraut Puff-Pie *(Sauerkrautpastete)*

Puff-Pie Crust (No. 343)
1½ lbs. cooked sauerkraut,
  dry
1 lb. frankfurters or bacon,
  lightly fried
1 cup cream (or milk)
3 tbls. Tomato Sauce
  (No. 284)
1 tbls. paprika
1 egg yolk

Prepare dough. Grease a baking dish and
line with two-thirds of the dough. Arrange alternate layers of cooked sauerkraut and frankfurters or bacon. Mix together cream, Tomato Sauce and paprika
and pour over casserole. Roll out remaining dough to fit across top of pie and
prick with fork to provide airholes. Or
dough may be cut in strips and laid on
top in any desired pattern. Brush top
dough with egg yolk. Bake in moderate
(350°) oven for one hour.
Serves 4.

345. Leftovers Pie *(Pastete aus Restgerichten)*

Puff-Pie Crust (No. 343)
¼ cup bread crumbs
2 lbs. beans, cooked
1 lb. roast lamb, sliced
gravy, 1 cup or less
1 egg yolk
Sauce:
1 cup cream
2 eggs
¼ cup vegetable juice
curry or garlic, to taste
1 tsp. onion, chopped
2 tbls. white wine
salt and pepper

Roll dough out thin and use most of it to
line greased baking dish. Sprinkle with
bread crumbs and fill with alternating
layers of beans, meat slices and gravy.
Prepare sauce, blending well, and pour
over pie-filling. Use remaining dough to
cover the pie, pricking with a fork for
airholes. Brush with egg yolk and bake
in a moderate oven (350°) for an hour.
Serves 4.

346. Deep Dish Pumpkin-and-Meat Pie
(Kürbispastete)

Puff-Pie Crust (No. 343)
bread crumbs
2 lbs. pumpkin
2 tbls. vinegar
¼ cup grated cheese
1 lb. meat, ground
salt and pepper
basil
½ cup cream
1 tbls. butter
1 egg yolk

Prepare dough, roll out and line a greased baking dish with it. Sprinkle with bread crumbs. Cube pumpkin meat, cover with water, add vinegar and cook until tender, 20 to 30 minutes. Drain. Arrange alternate layers of pumpkin, grated cheese and ground meat, ending with a layer of pumpkin. Season each layer well. Pour cream over filling, sprinkle with grated cheese and dot with butter. Roll out remaining dough, cut in strips and arrange decoratively on top. Brush with egg yolk and bake in moderate (350°) oven for about one hour.

Serves 4.

347. Fish in Its Own Juice
(Fischgericht im eigenen Saft)

2 lbs. fish fillets
lemon juice
2 tbls. butter
1 cup sour cream (or milk)
1 tbls. herbs, chopped
salt
paprika
grated cheese
bread crumbs

Sprinkle fish fillets with lemon juice and let stand. Melt butter in baking dish. Add fish, cover and steam for 10 minutes. Mix sour cream, herbs and seasoning well to form marinade. Pour over fish and steam another 10 minutes. Top with grated cheese and bread crumbs and bake in moderate (350°) oven until nicely browned. Serve with Salted Potatoes (No. 199) and Cucumber Salad (No. 244).

Serves 4.

348. Baked Kippers *(Bücklinge, überbacken)*

4 smoked kippers
4 tbls. sour cream
4 tbls. milk
2 tbls. bread crumbs
1 tbls. parsley, chopped
2 tbls. butter

Place kippers in cream in greased baking dish. Add milk, sprinkle with bread crumbs and parsley. Dot with butter. Bake in a moderate (375°) oven for about 10 minutes. Serve with Mashed Potatoes (No. 204) and Sauerkraut (No. 238).
Serves 4.

349. Fish with Macaroni
(Fischauflauf mit Makkaroni)

½ lb. macaroni
1 lb. smoked fish
1 tbls. flour
2 tbls. butter
½ to 1 cup milk
lemon juice
salt and pepper
2 tbls. bread crumbs
1 tbls. butter

Cook macaroni in salted water. Drain. Chop up fish. Grease baking dish and arrange layers of macaroni and fish. Pour over sauce made from flour and butter, thinned with milk and seasoned with lemon juice, salt and pepper. Sprinkle top with bread crumbs and dot with butter. Bake in a moderate (375°) oven until nicely browned, 15 to 20 minutes.
Serves 4.

350. Vegetarian Sandwiches
(Belegte Brote, vegetarisch)

bread
butter

(a)
radishes, sliced
cucumber, sliced
sour cream
parsley, chopped

(b)
tomatoes, sliced
hard-cooked eggs, sliced
chives, chopped

(c)
tomatoes, sliced
horseradish

(d)
lettuce, chopped
spinach, chopped
tomatoes, sliced
hard-cooked egg, sliced

Slices of rye, graham, dark bread or pumpernickel, spread generously with butter and topped with:

(a) Sliced radishes and cucumber dipped in sour cream and sprinkled with chopped parsley.

(b) Sliced tomatoes and hard-cooked eggs, garnished with chopped chives.

(c) Sliced tomatoes seasoned with prepared horseradish and salt.

(d) Chopped lettuce or spinach, covered with slices of tomato and hard-cooked egg.

351. Vegetable Platter (Gemüseplatte)

1 head cauliflower
6 tomatoes
1 head endive, chopped
2 tbls. olive oil
2 tbls. lemon juice
4 tbls. cream
1 tsp. honey
1 tsp. parsley and chives,
    chopped
pinch of salt

Separate cauliflower into flowerets and slice tomatoes. Arrange platter with cauliflower in center, surrounded by tomatoes; sprinkle with endive. Blend other ingredients into a smooth sauce and pour over all vegetables.

Serves 4.

352. Baked Mushrooms with Noodles
(Pilzauflauf mit Nudeln)

½ lb. noodles
1 lb. mushrooms
2 tbls. butter
salt and pepper
parsley, chopped
2 tbls. bread crumbs
1 tbl. butter

Cook and drain noodles. Slice mushrooms and sauté in butter 5 minutes. Season well. Add parsley. Arrange alternating layers of noodles and mushrooms in buttered baking dish, sprinkle with bread crumbs and dot with butter. Bake in 375° oven until golden brown, about 10 minutes.
Serves 4.

353. Potato and Tomato Casserole
(Kartoffeln mit Tomaten)

2 lbs. potatoes, cooked
1 lb. tomatoes, sliced
3 tbls. cheese, grated
salt and pepper
marjoram
1 onion, sliced and slightly
    fried
butter, to dot

Peel and slice potatoes. In a buttered baking dish, arrange alternating layers of potatoes, tomatoes and grated cheese. Sprinkle with salt, pepper and marjoram. Top with cheese and fried onion rings, dot with butter. Bake in moderate (350°) oven for 30 minutes.
Serves 4.

354. Snow Pancakes (Schneepfannkuchen)

2¼ cups flour
1 cup milk
3 eggs, separated
salt, nutmeg
1-2 tbls. butter

Prepare a thick batter from flour, milk, egg yolks and seasoning. Beat egg whites stiffly and fold in. Melt butter in skillet and fry small pancakes brown on both sides. Serve immediately on a hot platter.
Serves 4.

355. Spinach Pancakes (*Spinatpfannkuchen*)

½ lb. spinach
2 eggs
3 tbls. flour
1 cup milk
salt
2 tbls. butter

Wash spinach carefully, chop and mix with eggs, flour, milk and salt to form a smooth dough. Melt butter and fry pancakes until nicely browned on both sides. Serve with salads or with Tomato (No. 284) or Caper Sauce (No. 282). Serves 2.

356. Deep Fried Asparagus (*Gebackener Spargel*)

2 lbs. asparagus
salt
2 eggs, beaten
1-2 cups flour
fat

Cook asparagus in slightly salted water until half done. Chop off top half of stalks and tie together in bundles of 5 or 6. Dip in beaten egg and then roll in flour. Fry in deep fat. The stubs and cooking water can be used for soup. Serves 4.

357. Stuffed Tomatoes *(Gefüllte Tomaten)*

12 tomatoes

Rice Filling:
2 cups rice, cooked
2 tbls. butter
tomato pulp
salt and pepper
2 tbls. cheese, grated
extra butter

Cheese Filling:
2 tbls. flour
2 tbls. butter
tomato pulp
4 tbls. cheese, grated
1½ cups milk
2 eggs, separated

Cut off tops of tomatoes and scoop out pulp. Cook pulp down, strain and blend with desired filling:
Rice filling: Mix rice, butter, tomato pulp and seasonings. Stuff tomato shells with mixture, sprinkle with cheese, dot with butter. Either steam, covered, in butter or bake in moderate (350°) oven until well browned, 30 to 40 minutes.
Cheese filling: Brown flour in butter over low heat, add tomato pulp and cheese and moisten gradually with milk, blending well. Heat thoroughly but do not boil. Remove from heat and let cool. Stir in egg yolks, fold in beaten egg whites and stuff into tomato shells. Bake in moderate (350°) oven 30 to 40 minutes. Serve with green salad or vegetables.
Serves 6-12.

358. Stuffed Cucumbers *(Gurken, gefüllt)*

4 medium cucumbers or
    2 large cucumbers
4 rolls
1 cup milk
2 tbls. butter
1 tbls. onions, chopped
1 tsp. parsley, chopped
2 eggs, separated
salt and pepper
½ cup beef stock
4 slices bacon, cooked lightly
    or ¼ lb. ground meat,
    optional

Pare cucumbers, always cutting toward stem end. Cut in half lengthwise and scoop out insides. Soak rolls in milk, squeeze dry and pluck to pieces. Melt butter and sauté rolls, onions and parsley. Stir in egg yolks, seasoning and beef stock and fold in beaten egg whites. Stuffing may be enriched by adding crumbled bacon or ground meat, if desired.
Serves 4.

359.   Spinach Pudding *(Spinatpudding)*

1 lb. spinach
4 rolls
¼ cup milk
1 onion, chopped
1 tsp. parsley, chopped
4 tbls. butter
3 eggs, separated
salt
nutmeg

Wash, cook and drain spinach and pass through a strainer. Soak rolls in milk, squeeze dry and pluck to pieces. Sauté rolls, onions and parsley in butter. Add spinach and let simmer briefly. Remove from heat, stir in egg yolks and seasonings. Let cool. Fold in well-beaten egg whites. Pour into greased pudding form, set in water and cook over moderate heat for one hour. Serve with a spicy sauce and salads.
Serves 4.

360.   Cheese Pudding *(Käsepudding)*

6 tbls. butter
1 cup flour
¼ lb. cheese, grated
1 cup milk
4 eggs, separated
salt
nutmeg

Melt butter, add flour, stir in grated cheese. Thin with milk and cook briefly. Let cool. Stir in egg yolks, season well and fold in well-beaten egg whites. Turn into greased pudding form, cover, set in water and cook over moderate heat for 40 minutes. Serve with spinach.
Serves 4.

361.   Tomato Soufflé *(Tomatenauflauf)*

1½ lbs. tomatoes
1 cup milk
2 tbls butter
1 tsp. salt
1½ cups flour
2 eggs, separated
1 tbls. parsley, chopped
1 tsp. baking powder

Scald and peel tomatoes. Place upright in buttered baking dish. Bring to a boil the milk, butter and salt. Remove from heat and, when cool, stir in flour, egg yolks, parsley, baking powder. Fold in beaten egg whites. Season well, pour this sauce over tomatoes and bake in moderate (350°) oven for 30 minutes.
Serves 4.

362. Potato Soufflé (*Kartoffelauflauf*)

1 lb. potatoes
2 tbls. butter
3 tbls. sugar
2 eggs, separated
peel of ½ lemon, grated
pinch of salt

Cook, peel and mash potatoes the day before. Blend well butter, sugar and egg yolks and mix with potatoes. Beat egg whites stiffly and fold in. Add lemon peel and salt. Pour into greased baking dish and bake in 375° oven for 40 minutes
Serves 4.

DESSERTS AND SWEETS
(*Desserts und Süssspeisen*)

363. Dough Beignette—Basic Batter
(*Beignettenteig*)

2 cups flour
1 egg
2 tsp. sugar
1 pinch of salt
2 tbls. melted butter
1 jigger of rum
warm water
fruit of your choice

It is advisable to mix this batter several hours before using. Blend all ingredients and add enough warm water to form a creamy batter. Let cool. Dip slices of apples, bananas, pineapple or other fruits in this sweet batter. Fry in deep hot fat. (For vegetables, meat or fish, prepare an unsweetened batter by eliminating sugar and rum.)
Serves 4.

364.   Cherry Pancakes *(Kirschpfannkuchen)*

4 rolls
4 tbls. flour
2 eggs
1 cup milk
2 tsp. sugar
1 lb. cherries
butter or fat
cinnamon and sugar, mixed

Soak rolls in cold water, squeeze dry and break up. Mix rolls thoroughly with flour, eggs, milk and sugar. Pit cherries and fold into batter. Drop spoonfuls of batter in deep hot fat or sauté in butter. To serve, top with cinnamon and sugar. Serves 4.

365.   Rice in Milk *(Milchreis)*

1¼ cups rice
salt
4 cups milk
3 tbls. sugar
dash of vanilla or
   1 tsp. grated lemon peel
2 tbls. butter
2 tbls. powdered sugar
   and cinnamon

Cook rice in slightly salted water for 10 minutes. Drain, add milk and simmer 10 minutes more. Season. Stir in butter (or brown it and add). To serve, sprinkle with powdered sugar and cinnamon, blended. Serves 4.

366.   Rice Pancakes *(Reisschmarren)*

1 cup rice
2 cups milk
salt
4 tbls. butter
2 eggs, whole
2 egg yolks
2 tbls. almonds, chopped
2 tbls. raisins
2 tbls. currants, dried
butter for frying
powdered sugar and
   cinnamon, mixed

Cook rice in slightly salted milk 15 minutes. Let cool. Cream butter and fold in eggs and egg yolks. Blend this with lukewarm rice. Add almonds, raisins and currants. Melt butter in pan and fry mixture in it. As soon as bottom starts to brown, turn over. Repeat several times until well-browned on both sides. Sprinkle with cinnamon and sugar. Serve with stewed fruits. Serves 4.

367. Cream Strudel (*Rahmstrudel*)

2 cups flour
2 eggs
1 tbls. butter
⅓ cup lukewarm water
¼ tsp. vinegar
pinch of salt
2 tbls. butter
2 eggs, separated
4 tbls. sugar
1 cup sour cream
peel of ⅓ lemon, grated
¼ lb. cottage cheese
¼ lb. almonds, chopped
¼ lb. raisins
cinnamon
4 tbls. butter, melted

Put flour in a bowl and make depression in the center. Into this break the eggs. Add butter, water, vinegar and salt and work until tender. Dough must be firm and have air holes in it when cut. Brush with lukewarm water. Heat a large pot and place over dough for 30 minutes.

For the filling, cream butter, stir in egg yolks and sugar, add sour cream, grated lemon peel and smooth cottage cheese. Beat egg whites and fold in.

Sprinkle baking cloth with flour. Roll out dough as thin as possible; then stretch it by hand to paper thinness. Brush with melted butter. Heap on filling generously; top with chopped almonds, raisins and cinnamon. Lift baking cloth by one edge so that dough starts to roll up. Brush each turn with melted butter until dough is completely rolled up. Butter a baking sheet and carefully transfer roll to it. Press ends of roll flat. Brush entire strudel with melted butter. Bake in a hot (425°) oven 40 to 50 minutes.

Note: Strudel dough is, traditionally, pulled out by hand, by putting both hands, palm-side up under the dough and stretching as thin as possible. This is a perilous procedure for the uninitiated, so an alternate suggestion has been given: roll it out paper-thin.

368. Apple Strudel (*Apfelstrudel*)

2 cups flour
2 eggs, beaten
¼ cup water, lukewarm
pinch of salt
½ tsp. vinegar
4-5 lbs. apples, tart
⅓ cup sugar
3 tbls. cinnamon
6 tbls. butter, melted
4 tbls. bread crumbs
1 cup almonds or other
   nuts, chopped
1½ cups raisins

Heap flour on bread board and make a depression in the center large enough to hold the beaten egg, water, salt and vinegar. Knead this to a firm dough which, when cut, will reveal air pockets. Set dough, covered, in a warm place. Peel and grate apples and sprinkle with sugar and cinnamon. Dust a cloth with flour and on it roll out dough, the thinner the better. Melt butter, mix in bread crumbs, and coat dough. Spread out apples about 1 inch high on dough, sprinkle with almonds or other nuts, as desired, and raisins. Roll dough over, in the cloth, several times to form a loaf (strudel) of several alternating layers of dough and filling. Brush finished loaf with more melted butter, put on greased baking sheet and bake in a hot (400°) oven until crust is crisp and well browned. This may be served with Vanilla Sauce (No. 421).

369. Scrambled Pancakes (*Kaiserschmarren*)

2 tbls. butter
2 tbls. sugar
4 eggs, separated
1 pinch of salt
2 cups flour
1 cup milk or cream
2 tbls. butter

Cream butter until frothy. Then add, one after another, sugar, egg yolks, salt, flour and milk. Beat egg whites until stiff and carefully fold in. Melt butter in a pan and in it fry batter golden brown on each side. With two forks, chop up the resulting pancake. Serve on a hot platter, sprinkled with cinnamon and sugar and garnished with pieces of apple, cherries or other fruits, sautéed in butter, or with seedless raisins.

Serves 4.

370. Plum Dumplings (*Zwetschgenknödel*)

3 lbs. potatoes
5 cups flour
4 tbls. sugar
2 eggs, beaten
salt
4 tbls. butter, melted
2 lbs. plums
cubes of sugar
¼ cup bread crumbs
melted butter to dampen
cinnamon and sugar

Cook, peel and mash potatoes. Turn out on a floured bread board. Add flour, sugar, eggs, salt and melted butter and mix to form a firm dough. Roll out ½ inch thick and cut into pieces the size of your palm. Remove pits from plums and replace them with sugar cubes. Place one plum in each slice of dough. Fold dough around plums, to cover completely. Cook in slightly salted water 5 to 8 minutes. Mix crisp bread crumbs with melted butter. Roll finished dumplings in this and sprinkle with cinnamon and sugar.
Serves 4.

371. Raspberry Snow (*Himbeerschnee*)

1 qt. box raspberries
7 tbls. sugar
1 tbls. white wine
2 egg whites, beaten

Press raspberries through strainer. Add sugar and wine and blend well. Fold in stiffly beaten egg whites. Freeze until firm.
Serves 2.

372. Apple Snow (*Apfelschnee*)

1 lb. apples, quartered
4 tbls. sugar
1 tbls. lemon juice
2 egg whites, beaten

Stew unpeeled apples in a very little water, 10 to 15 minutes, then force through a strainer. Combine pulp with sugar and lemon juice. Fold in beaten egg whites. Set in ice and stir until quite thick. Serve with macaroons.
Serves 4.

373. Stuffed Apples (Gefüllte Äpfel)

4 large apples
4 tbls. raisins
3 tbls. sugar
1 tsp. cinnamon
1 tbls. bread crumbs
4 tbls. nuts, grated
2 tbls. butter
extra sugar
extra butter
1 cup white wine

Select apples of equal size, pare them and cut off tops. Scoop out cores carefully. Mix raisins, sugar, cinnamon, bread crumbs and nuts. Into each apple put first a piece of butter the size of a hazelnut, then the raisin and nut mixture. Replace tops and set in buttered baking dish. Sprinkle with sugar, dot with butter and pour on wine. Bake in moderate (350°) oven until soft, 30 to 40 minutes. Serves 4.

374. Apples in Nightgowns (Äpfel im "Schlafrock")

4 large apples
Mellow Dough, Sweet (No. 449) or Laminated Dough (No. 451)
4 tbls. almonds, grated
2 tbls. raisins
2 tbls. sugar
2 tbls. bread crumbs
pinch of cinnamon
2 tbls. butter
1 egg yolk, beaten
extra sugar

Pare and core apples. Prepare dough. Mix together almonds, raisins, sugar, bread crumbs and cinnamon. Put butter the size of a hazelnut in each hollow center and fill up with stuffing. Roll dough out thin and cut in squares large enough to enfold apples. Place apples in center of dough squares, lift up corners and press tightly together. Set apples on buttered baking sheet, brush with egg yolk and bake in moderate (350°) oven for 30 minutes. Sprinkle with sugar to serve. Serves 4.

375. Orange Biscuit *(Orangenbiskuit)*

4 oranges
5 tbls. sugar
1 jigger cognac
2 tbls. cornstarch
1 cup white wine
4 eggs, separated
12 sweet biscuits or 8 slices
    of sponge cake

Slice and seed 3 oranges, sprinkle with some sugar and let stand for 30 minutes. Pour on cognac. Drain liquid into a saucepan and add juice of remaining orange. Dissolve cornstarch in white wine, stir in sugar and egg yolks. Add this mixture to orange juice. Bring to a boil, stirring constantly. Cool slightly and fold in stiffly beaten egg whites. Butter a pudding form and lay out sweet biscuits or sponge cake and over this pour orange jelly mixture. Cover and cook in double boiler over moderate heat for 30 minutes. Chill, turn out, and decorate with orange slices.

Serves 4-6.

376. Biscuit Fanny *(Biskuit Lisette)*

small sponge cake
¼ lb. butter
3 egg yolks
5 tbls. confectioner's sugar
4 tbls. coffee extract
2 tbls. almonds, chopped

Cut sponge cake in strips. Cream butter, stir in egg yolks and sugar. Add coffee extract (or double strength coffee) drop by drop and continue stirring to a froth. Arrange strips of sponge cake crosswise, like a log pile, and cover with coffee mixture. Sprinkle with almonds.

Serves 4.

377. Fruit Rice (*Reis Trautmannsdorff*)

¾ cup rice
2 cups milk
½ tsp. vanilla extract
3 tbls. sugar
1 envelope gelatine
2 tbls. rum or cognac
1 cup cream, whipped
stewed fruits

Cook long-grain rice 20 minutes, drain well and cook again briefly in milk and vanilla. Dissolve sugar and gelatine in rum or cognac and stir into rice. Fold in whipped cream. Turn into a pudding ring, hollow in the middle, and chill. Turn out and serve garnished with peaches, apricots or sour cherries. Serves 4.

378. Lemon Rice (*Zitronenreis*)

½ cup rice
4 tbls. sugar
juice of 2 lemons
peel of ½ lemon, grated
pinch of salt
stewed fruits

Cook rice in water, adding sugar, lemon juice, lemon peel and salt. When rice is done (about 20 minutes) drain, turn into a moistened pudding ring, hollow in center, and chill. Turn out on a glass platter and arrange fruits in center of ring. Save the juice of stewed fruits for a refreshing drink. Serves 4.

379. Apples Charlotte (*Äpfel Charlotte*)

½ lb. butter
4 French rolls, sliced
2 lbs. apples
1 tsp. lemon juice
¼ tsp. cinnamon
1 cup sugar
2 tbls. raisins, chopped
extra sugar

Melt half the butter and pour over thin slices of rolls. Lay half the slices out on a greased round cake pan. Peel, core and coarsely grate the apples. Stew in remaining butter, with lemon juice, cinnamon, sugar and raisins, until soft. Pour over bread in pan and cover with another layer of bread. Bake 45 minutes in moderate (350°) oven, turn out, sprinkle with sugar and serve. Serves 4-6.

380. Stuffed Oranges *(Gefüllte Orangen)*

6 oranges
4 egg yolks
¾ cup sugar
juice of 2 oranges
peel of ½ orange, grated
2 tbls. lemon juice
1 envelope gelatine,
      dissolved
4 egg whites, beaten, or
      1 cup cream, whipped

Cut tops off oranges and scoop out inside sections with a silver spoon. Combine egg yolks and sugar and stir for 15 minutes. Add orange juice, grated orange peel, lemon juice and gelatine. Fold in either beaten egg whites or whipped cream. Fill orange shells with this mixture and chill for 3 hours. Garnish with orange sections and whipped cream. Serves 6.

381. Strawberries Elizabeth *(Erdbeeren Elizabeth)*

1 qt. strawberries
7 tbls. sugar
2 tbls. cognac
1 envelope gelatine
2 cups cream, whipped

Mash strawberries (retaining a few whole to garnish) and mix with sugar and cognac. Dissolve gelatine and stir into mixture. Fold in whipped cream. Chill. To serve, turn out on platter and decorate with more whipped cream and a few whole strawberries. Serves 4.

382. Strawberries with Whipped Cream *(Erdbeeren mit Schlagrahm)*

6″ sponge cake, sliced, or
      macaroons
1 qt. strawberries, fresh
2 tbls. sugar
1½ tbls. water
1 cup cream, whipped

Place alternate layers of cake and strawberries in a glass bowl. Cook sugar in water, add a few berries. Strain and cool. Whip cream and fold in the dissolved sugar. Heap on strawberries to serve. This may also be applied to apricots, peaches or sour cherries. Serves 4.

383. Chestnut Plombière *(Kastanien-Plombière)*

1:
2 cups milk, hot
¼ cup sugar
5 egg yolks
pinch of salt
2 cups cream
2 tbls. cognac
1 tbls. vanilla-sugar (sugar
  that has been stored
  with a vanilla bean)

2:
1 envelope gelatine
2 tbls. cold water
2¼ cups cream
⅓ cup confectioner's sugar
¼ cup raisins
1½ tbls. cognac
10 chestnuts, roasted and
  shelled
5 macaroons
1 tsp. vanilla
pinch of salt

1: Combine first four ingredients, and in a double boiler over moderate heat, stir until mixture thickens. Strain and chill. Stir in cream and chill further. Finally fold in cognac and vanilla-sugar and freeze 2 hours, stirring twice during the process.

2: Dissolve gelatine in water and add ¼ cup of the cream, warmed; stir in confectioner's sugar. Chill. Soak raisins for 1 hour in cognac. Chop up chestnuts and macaroons and combine all foregoing ingredients with the remaining whipped cream, the vanilla and salt.

Arrange alternate layers of 1 and 2 in a mold and put in freezing compartment for 2 hours.

Serves 6.

SOUFFLÉS AND PUDDINGS

384. Rice Soufflé *(Reisauflauf)*

1 cup rice
3 cups milk, hot
pinch of salt
2 tbls. butter
4 tbls. sugar
peel of ¼ lemon
3 eggs, separated
2 tbls. raisins
butter, to dot

Cook rice in lightly salted water 10 minutes. Drain, add hot milk and salt and finish cooking over low heat, about 15 minutes. Let cool. Cream butter, stir in sugar, grated lemon peel and egg yolks. To this add rice and raisins. Fold in well-beaten egg whites. Transfer to greased baking dish. Dot with butter and bake in hot (425°) oven for 30 minutes. Serve with stewed fruits, berries or fruit juice.
Serves 4.

385.   Apple-Rice with Snow Cap
(Apfelreis mit Schneehaube)

1 cup rice
2 cups milk
2 tbls. butter
3 tbls. sugar
peel of ⅓ lemon, grated
3 eggs, separated
5 tart apples
3 tbls. raisins
⅓ cup confectioner's sugar

Cook rice in slightly salted milk. Cream butter, flavor with sugar and grated lemon peel. Fold in egg yolks. Add rice and mix well. Pare and slice apples, sprinkle with raisins and add to other ingredients. Transfer to greased baking dish. Beat egg whites and fold in confectioner's sugar. Top rice mixture with a mound of sweetened egg whites and bake in 375° oven until well browned, 10 to 15 minutes.

Serves 4.

386.   Tapioca Soufflé (Sagoauflauf)

1 cup tapioca
3 cups milk
pinch of salt
2 tbls. butter
⅓ cup sugar
2 eggs, separated
1⅓ tbls. lemon juice
1 tsp. baking soda

Soak tapioca pearls overnight. Cook tapioca in salted milk until it thickens. Or use quick-cooking tapioca. Let it cool. Cream butter, stir in sugar, egg yolks and lemon juice. Combine with tapioca, and when cool, fold in beaten egg whites and baking soda. Bake in a greased baking dish in moderately hot (375°) oven for 30 minutes.

Serves 4.

387. Almond or Poppy Seed Soufflé (*Semmelauflauf*)

6 rolls
1 cup milk
5 tbls. butter
1 cup sugar
3 eggs, separated
peel of ¼ lemon, grated
1¼ tbls. lemon juice
1 cup almonds or poppy seeds
¼ cup raisins

Slice rolls and soak in milk until it is absorbed. Cream butter, stir in sugar, egg yolks, lemon peel and juice. Shred almonds and fold almonds (or poppy seeds), raisins, soaked rolls and stiffly beaten egg whites into butter mixture. Bake in a greased baking dish, in a hot oven (425°), for 30 minutes.
Serves 4.

388. Chocolate Soufflé (*Schokolade Auflauf*)

2 tbls. butter
2 tbls. flour
¼ cup milk
3 eggs, separated
1¼ squares chocolate
⅓ cup sugar
2 tbls. water, hot
¼ tsp. vanilla

Melt butter, add flour. Gradually stir in milk and bring to a boil. Add egg yolks. Melt chocolate in double boiler, add sugar and water and stir until smooth. Combine the two and let cool. Fold in well-beaten egg whites and flavor with vanilla. Butter a baking dish, pour in mixture and bake in moderate (350°) oven for 25 minutes. Serve with Vanilla Cream Sauce (No. 428).
Serves 4-6.

389. Nut Soufflé *(Nussauflauf)*

1 cup flour
1½ cups milk
5 tbls. butter
pinch of salt
4 eggs, separated
5 tbls. sugar
1 cup nuts, grated

Stir flour into ½ cup of milk. Bring to a boil remaining milk, butter and salt. Remove from heat, add flour mixture, mixing well, and let cool. Blend in egg yolks, sugar and nuts. Carefully fold in beaten egg whites. Pour into buttered baking dish and bake in 350° oven for an hour. Serve hot, with Vanilla (No. 421) or Chocolate Sauce (No. 424).
Serves 4.

390. Raspberry Soufflé *(Himbeer Soufflé)*

Pastry Cream (No. 412)
1 cup raspberries, fresh
sugar to taste
6 egg whites, beaten
sugar and butter

Prepare cream and chill. Stew raspberries in a little water, 5 minutes. Drain and press through strainer. Add sugar to taste to pulp and cook until syrupy. Stir into cream. Fold in egg whites. Pour into buttered baking dish, sprinkled with sugar, and bake in hot (425°) oven for 12 minutes.
Serves 4.

391. Lemon Soufflé *(Zitronen Soufflé)*

4 eggs, separated
1 cup sugar
2 tbls. lemon juice
peel of 1 lemon, grated

Stir egg yolks until frothy and gradually add sugar, lemon juice and grated peel. Fold in stiffly beaten whites. Pour into buttered baking dish and bake in a moderate oven (350°) for 25 minutes.
Serves 2.

392. Orange Soufflé (*Orangenauflauf*)

2 oranges, peel and juice
1½ cups milk
6 tbls. flour
4 tbls. butter
6 eggs, separated
8 tbls. sugar

Peel the outer part of one orange with a very sharp knife and bring peel to a boil in 1 cup of milk. Let stand for flavor to permeate milk. Mix flour in remaining milk. Remove peels and add flour mixture to milk. Stir over low heat until it begins to thicken. Cream butter, stir in egg yolks, sugar and juice from peeled oranges. Fold in beaten egg whites. Pour into buttered baking dish and bake in moderate (350°) oven about 35 minutes, until golden brown.

Serves 4.

393. Apple Soufflé (*Apfelauflauf*)

1 lb. apples
sugar and cinnamon
1 tbls. raisins
1 tbls. butter
2 eggs
1 cup milk
1 tbls. cornstarch
1 tbls. sugar
1 tbls. almonds, grated
extra butter

Pare and core apples and slice thinly. Place slices in buttered baking dish with a little water, sprinkle with sugar, cinnamon and raisins, dot with butter. Cover and stew until tender. Combine eggs, milk, cornstarch and sugar, stirring thoroughly, and pour over apples. Sprinkle with grated almonds, dot with butter, and bake in moderate (350°) oven about 35 minutes, until golden brown.

Serves 4.

394.   Cottage Cheese Soufflé *(Quarkauflauf)*

4 tbls. butter
4 eggs, separated
1 cup sugar
1 lb. cottage cheese
1 cup cream
4 tbls. cornstarch
peel of ½ lemon, grated
3 tbls. raisins
1 tsp. vanilla
2 tbls. almonds, grated

Cream butter, add egg yolks and sugar and stir to a froth. Strain cottage cheese and blend with cream. Add this little by little to butter mixture and beat until firm and light. Fold in cornstarch, lemon peel, raisins, vanilla and beaten egg whites. Pour into buttered baking dish, sprinkle with almonds and bake in moderate (350°) oven about 50 minutes. Serves 4.

395.   Noodle Pudding *(Nudelauflauf)*

¾ lb. broad noodles
3 eggs
2 tbls. butter
1 cup milk
¼ cup vanilla-sugar (sugar stored with a vanilla bean) or add a dash of vanilla to plain sugar

Cook noodles, rinse, drain and transfer to greased baking dish. Blend thoroughly all other ingredients and pour over noodles. Dot with butter and bake in moderate oven (350°) for 30 minutes. Serve with stewed fruits or berries. Serves 4.

396.   Fruit Pudding *(Obstauflauf)*

2 cups milk
4 tbls. sugar
cinnamon
peel of ¼ lemon, grated, or dash of vanilla
1 loaf bread
1 lb. fresh fruit, such as strawberries, raspberries, cherries or oranges

Sweeten milk and flavor with cinnamon, lemon peel or vanilla. Slice bread and soak briefly in milk. In a greased baking dish, arrange alternate layers of bread and fruit. Bake in 375° oven for 30 minutes. Serves 4.

397. Apple Beggar ("*Apfelbettelmann*")

1 lb. apples
2 tbls. sugar
10-12 slices brown bread,
  grated
2 tbls. butter
1 tsp. cinnamon
peel of ½ lemon, grated
1 tbls. almonds, grated
1 tbls. raisins
butter, to dot

Peel, core and slice apples thinly. Cook in scant ½ cup water with 1 tablespoon sugar. Fry bread lightly in butter, mix in remaining sugar, cinnamon, grated lemon peel, almonds and raisins. Grease baking dish. Place half of bread mixture in it. Add stewed apples and top with remaining bread. Dot with butter and bake in 400° oven about 10 minutes, until well browned. To serve, sprinkle with cinnamon and sugar.

Serves 4.

398. Semolina Pudding (*Griessflammeri*)

2 cups milk
3 tbls. sugar
pinch of salt
5 tbls. of semolina
peel of ½ lemon, grated
1 tbls. raisins, chopped
1 tbls. candied lemon
  peel, chopped
1 egg, separated

Heat milk, sugar and salt. Stir in semolina and cook for 10 minutes. Mix in grated lemon peel, raisins and candied lemon peel. Remove from heat. Stir in egg yolk, then fold in stiffly beaten egg white. Rinse glass dish and pour in mixture while dish is moist. Chill and, to serve, turn out on a platter. Serve with Fruit Sauce (No. 429).

Serves 3.

399. Almond Pudding *(Mandelflammeri)*

2 tbls. cornstarch
1 cup milk
2 tbls. sugar
pinch of salt
1 tbls. chopped almonds
1 tbls. butter
1 egg, separated

Stir cornstarch in a little milk until smooth. Bring to a boil the rest of the milk, sugar, salt and almonds. Add cornstarch mixture and let cook for 3 minutes, stirring constantly. Remove from heat and stir in butter and egg yolk. Fold in stiffly beaten white. Rinse a glass dish, and while still moist, turn pudding into this, and chill.

Serves 2.

400. Chocolate Pudding, Chilled *(Schokoladeflammeri)*

2 cups milk
4 tbls. sugar
pinch of salt
4 tbls. cocoa
1 envelope gelatine
1 egg, separated

Heat one cup of milk and dissolve sugar and salt in it. Stir cocoa and gelatine in second cup of cold milk. Combine the two mixtures and, stirring constantly, cook together about 3 minutes until thickened. Remove from heat. Stir in egg yolk and fold in beaten white. Rinse glass dish and pour in mixture while dish is moist. Chill, then turn out on platter to serve. Serve with Vanilla Sauce (No. 421).

Serves 4.

401. Chocolate Pudding, Hot (*Schokoladepudding*)

1½ squares chocolate
2 cups milk
3 tbls. butter
dash of vanilla
1¼ cups flour
6 tbls. sugar
4 eggs, separated

Melt chocolate and stir into 1 cup of milk. Add butter and vanilla to second cup of milk and bring to a boil. Combine mixtures, add flour and let cool. Add sugar and egg yolks and stir for 20 minutes. Fold in beaten whites. Transfer to buttered pudding form, cover, set in water and cook over moderate heat for 1 hour. Turn out to serve, hot, with Vanilla Sauce (No. 421).
Serves 4-6.

402. Cabinet Pudding (*Kabinettpudding*)

6″ square sponge cake
raspberry or apricot jam
3 eggs
1 cup milk
dash of vanilla
2 tbls. sugar

Split sponge cake in half and spread with jam; put together like a jam sandwich. Cut in cubes. Butter a pudding form and set cubes in it. Stir eggs in milk, add vanilla and sugar and pour over cubes. Cover, set in water, and cook over moderate heat for 40 minutes. Turn out on platter and serve hot, with Vanilla (No. 421) or Wine Sauce (No. 426).
Serves 4.

403. Bread Pudding *(Brotpudding)*

10 slices white bread
10 slices brown bread
6 tbls. sugar
3 cups milk
2 tbls. butter
1 tbls. flour
1 tbls. raisins, chopped
3 tbls. candied lemon peel,
      chopped
1 cup almonds, chopped
2 tbls. rum
confectioner's sugar

Break bread into small pieces. Dissolve sugar in milk and soak bread in this for 1 hour. Melt butter, mix with bread and blend in flour, raisins, lemon peel and nuts. Transfer to pudding form, cover, set in water and cook over moderate heat for 20 minutes. Turn out and sprinkle with rum and sugar to serve. Or serve with Wine (No. 426) Fruit (No. 429) or Vanilla Sauce (No. 421).
Serves 4-6.

404. Lemon Pudding *(Zitronenpudding)*

¼ lb. butter
peel of 1 lemon, grated
3 tbls. lemon juice
3 eggs
1 cup sugar
8 thin slices bread
2 eggs
3 tbls. sugar
pinch of salt
1 cup milk
peel of 1 lemon, grated

Cook together butter, lemon peel and juice for 2 minutes. Beat eggs lightly and add. Add sugar and cook until mixture thickens. Cool. Soak bread in this. Butter pudding form and lay bread in it. Beat eggs lightly. Add sugar, salt, milk and grated lemon peel. Pour this over bread. Cover form, set in water and cook over moderate heat for 1 hour.
Serves 4.

405. Cherry Pudding (*Kirschpudding*)

2¼ cups bread crumbs or zweiback, crumbled
2 cups milk
4 tbls. sugar
2 eggs, separated
3 tbls. almonds, chopped
pinch of cinnamon
1 lb. cherries, sour, pitted
1 tsp. baking powder
1 tsp. flour

Soak bread crumbs or zweiback in milk. Mix sugar and egg yolks, add almonds and cinnamon and blend well. Add this to bread crumbs. Combine cherries, flour and baking powder, fold in beaten egg whites, and add. Transfer to buttered pudding form, cover, set in water and cook over moderate heat for 1½ hours. Serve with Vanilla Sauce (No. 421).
Serves 4-6.

JELLIES (*Geleespeisen*)

406. Almond Jelly (*Mandelgelee*)

2 cups milk
¼ cup almonds, grated
7 tbls. sugar
1 envelope gelatine

Bring to a boil and cook briefly together the milk, almonds and sugar. Remove from heat. Dissolve gelatine and stir in. Pour into mold and chill. This may be turned out on a dessert platter to serve.
Serves 4.

407. Orange or Lemon Jelly (*Orangen-oder Zitronengelee*)

1 cup white wine
juice of 2 oranges
juice of 1 lemon
peel of 1 orange, grated
peel of 1 lemon, grated
3 tbls. sugar
1 envelope gelatine

Measure wine and juice together and, if necessary, add water to provide 2 cups of liquid. Stir in peels and sugar and bring to a boil. Remove from heat. Dissolve gelatine and stir in. Turn into glass dish and chill. Serve with whipped cream or Vanilla Cream Deluxe (No. 413).
Serves 4.

408. Wine Jelly (*Weingelee*)

¼ cup white wine
¼ cup water
2 tbls. sugar
1 tsp. lemon juice
¼ envelope gelatine

Bring to a boil the wine, water, sugar and lemon juice. Remove from heat, let cool. Dissolve gelatine and stir in. Rinse glass dish and pour in liquid while dish is wet. Chill. Turn out on dessert platter to serve. Serves 2.

409. Red Berry Jelly (*Rote Grütze*)

¼ lb. raspberries, fresh
½ lb. currants, fresh
1 pint wine
7 tbls. sugar
1 envelope gelatine

Cook berries briefly in the wine. Force through strainer. Add sugar to the pulp and bring to a boil again. Dissolve gelatine in fruit juice, stir into mixture and cook for about 3 minutes. Rinse glass dish, leaving it moist, and pour in jelly. Chill and serve with whipped cream or Vanilla Sauce (No. 421). Serves 4.

CREAMS (*Cremes*)

410. Whipped Cream (*Schlagrahm*)

2 cups whipping cream
2 tbls. sugar
pinch of vanilla-sugar (sugar
    stored with a vanilla
    bean) or add a dash of
    vanilla to plain sugar

Pour cream into a bowl, set in ice and beat steadily in one direction until it is stiff. Sweeten with sugar and vanilla-sugar, and beat again briefly. Serve cold, in a glass bowl, decorated with fruit as desired.

411. False Whipped Cream (*Falscher Schlagrahm*)

2 cups milk
2 tbls. sugar
dash of vanilla
1 tbls. flour or cornstarch

Bring 1 cup of milk, the sugar and vanilla to a boil. Remove from heat. Stir flour or cornstarch into second cup of milk. Combine both mixtures and cook over moderate heat, stirring constantly, for 3 to 5 minutes. Cool and chill overnight. Just before serving, beat until stiff.

412. Pastry Cream (*Creme Patissière*)

vanilla bean
1 cup milk
2 egg yolks
1 whole egg
8 tbls. sugar
3 tbls. flour

Cook vanilla bean in milk about 10 minutes, remove bean. In a double boiler, beat egg yolks, egg and sugar to a froth. Stir in flour. Continue beating while gradually adding hot milk until mixture is the consistency of mayonnaise. Serve hot. Cream may be used to stuff pancakes or as the basic batter for soufflés. Fruit extracts or liqueurs may be substituted for vanilla flavoring.

413. Vanilla Cream De Luxe (*Einfache Vanillecreme*)

vanilla bean
2 cups milk
1 tsp. cornstarch
4 egg yolks
7 tbls. sugar
1 envelope gelatine,
    dissolved
1 cup cream, whipped

Cook vanilla bean in ½ cup of milk. Remove bean. To remaining milk add cornstarch and vanilla-flavored milk and bring to a boil. Beat egg yolks and sugar to a froth and add. Stir in gelatine. Remove from heat and continue stirring until cream thickens. Fold in whipped cream, chill, and serve, in a glass bowl, with cookies.
Serves 4.

414. Chocolate Cream *(Schokoladecreme)*

1 egg yolk
2 tbls. sugar
1½ ozs. chocolate, grated
3 tbls. coffee, very strong
1 cup cream, whipped

Stir egg yolk and sugar to a froth. Melt chocolate, blend in coffee, combine with egg yolk. Beat thoroughly, fold in whipped cream, and chill. To serve, decorate with whipped cream.
Serves 2.

415. Madeira Cream *(Creme Nesselrode)*

5 egg yolks
1 tbls. sugar
2 jiggers Madeira wine
1 cup cream, whipped

Stir egg yolks, sugar and Madeira in double boiler, over low heat, until thick. Chill. Fold in whipped cream and serve in glass bowl with macaroons or cookies. Serves 4.

416. Hazelnut Cream *(Haselnusscreme)*

½ cup hazelnuts, shelled
1 cup milk
2 egg yolks
¼ cup sugar
vanilla
½ envelope gelatine,
    dissolved
½ cup cream, whipped

Heat hazelnuts in oven until brown skins peel. Rub in towel to remove skins. Grate. Combine with milk, egg yolks, sugar and vanilla and bring *almost* to a boil. Remove from heat and fold in dissolved gelatine. Gently stir until mixture thickens, then fold in whipped cream. Chill. Serve in glass bowl, decorated with whipped cream.
Serves 2.

417. Ginger Cream (*Ingwercreme*)

1 cup milk
2 egg yolks
¼ cup sugar
pinch of salt
½ envelope gelatine, dissolved
¼ cup Canton ginger, minced
3 tbls. ginger juice
1 tsp. vanilla
1 cup cream, whipped

In double boiler, over moderate heat, stir milk, egg yolks, sugar and salt and let come to a boil. Remove from heat. Add gelatine. Chill. When mixture begins to thicken, stir in ginger, ginger juice and vanilla, and fold in whipped cream.
Serves 4.

418. Wine Cream (*Weincreme*)

2 cups sherry or white wine
1 cup water
8 tbls. sugar
5 eggs
juice of ½ lemon
peel of ½ lemon, grated

Stir all ingredients to a thick froth in double boiler over low heat. Pour into sherbert glasses and chill before serving. This may be poured over slices of sponge cake and served either hot or cold.
Serves 4.

419. Chestnut Cream (*Kastaniencreme*)

2 lbs. chestnuts
2 cups milk
3 tbls. sugar
1 tsp. vanilla
1 cup cream

Cut chestnut shells crosswise, sprinkle with oil and bake in hot oven until shells will come off easily, about 10 minutes. It is desirable to shell them while hot. Remove brown skins. Heat milk, sugar and vanilla. Add chestnuts and cook until tender, 15 to 20 minutes. Put through strainer and stir into cream. Continue stirring over low heat until cream seems to have evaporated. Strain again. Serve on platter decorated with whipped cream.
Serves 4.

420.   Coffee Cream (*Kaffeecreme*)

½ cup double-strength coffee
½ cup cream (or milk)
2½ tbls. sugar
2 tbls. cornstarch
1 egg, separated

To the coffee add cream, or milk, and sugar and bring to a boil. Dissolve cornstarch in water, stir into mixture, and let it cook for 3 minutes. Remove from heat. Stir in beaten egg yolk and once more bring to a boil. Fold in beaten egg white, pour into glass bowl and chill thoroughly. Decorate with whipped cream just before serving.
Serves 2.

SWEET SAUCES (*Süsse Saucen*)

421.   Vanilla Sauce (*Vanillesauce*)

1 cup milk
1 tsp. vanilla
1 tbls. sugar
2 egg yolks
¼ tsp. cornstarch

Heat the milk and vanilla and then let cool. Blend sugar, egg yolks and cornstarch until smooth and stir into milk. Beat in double boiler over moderate heat until mixture thickens. Remove from heat and stir until cool.

422.   Almond Sauce (*Mandelsauce*)

1 cup milk
½ cup almonds, grated
2 egg yolks
2 tbls. sugar
¼ tsp. vanilla

Combine all ingredients and heat until thick in double boiler over moderate heat.

423. Caramel Sauce (*Karamelsauce*)

4 tbls. sugar
1 tbls. water
2 cups milk
1 tbls. cornstarch
1 egg, separated
½ tsp vanilla

Brown sugar lightly in a skillet. Add water and milk and bring to a boil. Dissolve cornstarch in water, add and cook 3 minutes. Thicken this mixture with egg yolk, flavor with vanilla and let cool. Just before serving fold in beaten egg white.

424. Chocolate Sauce (*Schokoladensauce*)

1 cup milk
2 tbls. sugar
1 tbls. cocoa (or chocolate, grated)
1 egg, separated

Blend all ingredients except egg white and beat until thick in double boiler over moderate heat. Cool, then fold in beaten egg white.

425. Arrack Sauce (*Arraksauce*)

1 cup white wine
2 eggs
4 tbls. sugar
1 jigger arrack

Heat wine, eggs and sugar to a froth over low heat. Add arrack and keep stirring until well blended.

426. Wine Sauce (*Weinsauce*)

1 cup white wine
2 eggs, whole
1 egg yolk
3 tbls. sugar
peel of ½ lemon, chopped
juice of ½ lemon

Combine all ingredients in an enamel pan and heat, over moderate flame, until thick. Do not boil. Serve either hot or cold.

427. Santa Monica Sauce *(Santa Monikasauce)*

1 tbls. butter
1 tbls. flour
¼ cup sugar
pinch of salt
½ cup milk
1 egg yolk
1 banana, mashed
½ cup cream, whipped

Cream butter and add flour, sugar and salt. Heat milk and let cool. Stir in egg yolk. Add milk and egg yolk gradually to batter and cook for 3 minutes over moderate heat. Cool and fold in banana and whipped cream.

428. Vanilla Cream Sauce *(Cremesauce)*

¼ cup butter
¾ cup confectioner's sugar
2 tbls. milk, warm
2 tbls. white wine
vanilla

Cream butter and beat sugar into it. Gradually add milk, wine and vanilla to taste. Stir until smooth.

429. Fruit Sauce *(Fruchtsauce)*

1 pt. raspberries or straw-
    berries or
  ½ lb. fresh fruit
½ to 1 cup sugar
2 cups water
1 tbls. cornstarch
2 tbls. wine

Cook berries, or fruit of your choice, with sugar in water until soft. Put through a sieve. Mix cornstarch and wine (or water) and stir into the hot syrup. Cook together for several minutes. Remove from heat. Fruit syrup may be used instead of fresh fruit, in which case, cut down on sugar accordingly.

YEAST BAKING *(Hefegebäck)*

430. Basic Raised Dough *(Vorteig)*

1¼ cups milk or water
1 yeast cake
¼ tsp. sugar
4 cups flour

Scald milk and let cool until lukewarm. Dissolve yeast in milk, add sugar. Stir in enough flour to make a fluid batter, the consistency of thick pancake batter. Cover and let rise for several hours until it has doubled in bulk. This preliminary batter is called the "rising." To the rising, add the rest of the flour (and at this point any other ingredients called for in each specific recipe, such as butter, eggs, sugar, salt, flavoring and, if necessary, additional lukewarm milk). Knead and beat dough thoroughly until it is satiny and comes away from sides of bowl and off hands easily. Grease bowl, set dough in it, grease top of dough to keep it soft, cover, set in a warm place and let rise again to double its size. Form into rolls, loaves or cake, as called for in specific recipe. Let rise 1 hour and bake in 375° oven 40 to 60 minutes. Bake rolls in 425° oven until nicely browned (about 25 minutes).
Note: This basic recipe makes 12 large rolls or 1 large loaf of bread. For bread or rolls, add ½ tsp. salt.

431. Poppy Rolls (*Mohnbrötchen*)

Basic Raised Dough
(No. 430)
½ tsp. salt
1 egg yolk, beaten
poppy or caraway seeds

Follow procedure and ingredients in above recipe, using salt instead of sugar. After final rising, shape into rolls, place on greased baking sheet and let rise again. Brush with egg yolk, sprinkle generously with poppy or caraway seeds. Bake in moderately hot (375°) oven until nicely browned, about 20 minutes.

432. Butter Crescents (*Butterhörnchen*)

1½ cups milk
½ yeast cake
½ tsp. salt
4 cups flour
6 tbls. butter

Scald ½ cup of milk and cool to luke-warm. Dissolve yeast in it. Add salt and enough flour to make a smooth batter. Cover and let rise for 1 hour. Add remaining milk and flour and 3 tablespoons butter and work to a tender dough. Cover and let rise 2 more hours. Divide dough into 20 or 25 parts and roll out into thin ovals. Brush with melted butter, fold over and bend into form of crescents. Place on greased baking sheet and let rise. Brush with water and bake in hot (400°) oven until golden brown, about 15 to 20 minutes. While still hot, and just before serving, brush with melted butter.

433. Yeast Braid *(Hefekranz)*

1½ cups milk
1 yeast cake
½ tsp. sugar
4 cups flour
¼ lb. butter
1 tbls. pork fat
¾ cup sugar
1 tsp. salt
2 eggs
½ lemon, juice and grated
peels
1 egg yolk
10 almonds, grated

Prepare a "rising" from milk, yeast, sugar and flour (see No. 430). Heat all additional ingredients (except egg yolk and almonds) briefly and add. Knead dough well until it comes easily off hands and away from sides of bowl. If necessary, add more milk but take care that dough is not too soft. Beat and knead until it blisters, cover and let rise in a warm place. Sprinkle baking board with flour, divide dough in three equal parts and lay alongside one another. Braid the three strands, beginning in the center and working toward the ends. Grease baking sheet, and place braid on it, shaped either in a ring or a horseshoe. If round, set a greased round can in the center to hold braid in shape. Sprinkle sugar on joints of braid, let it rise, brush with egg yolk, sprinkle with almonds and bake in a hot (400°) oven for 30 to 45 minutes, until nicely browned.

434. Almond Garland *(Marzipankranz)*

Dough:
1½ cups milk
1 yeast cake
4 cups flour
2 egg yolks
4 tbls. butter
4 tbls. sugar
1 tsp. salt
peel of ½ lemon, grated

Stuffing:
2 cups almonds, grated
1 cup confectioner's sugar
2 egg whites
dash of almond extract
2-3 tbls. raisins

Vanilla Icing (No. 454)

Prepare a "rising" from milk, yeast and flour (see No. 430). Heat other dough ingredients briefly and add. Knead dough well until it comes easily off hands and away from sides of bowl. If necessary, add more milk but take care that dough is not too soft. Beat and knead until it blisters, cover and let rise in a warm place. Beat almonds, sugar, egg whites and almond extract to a smooth consistency. Roll dough out thin to form a rectangle, brush with melted butter, spread with almond mixture, and sprinkle with raisins. Roll up tightly, then cut lengthwise in half. Shape halves into garlands, being careful stuffing does not drop out. Place on greased baking sheet and let rise. Bake in fairly hot (375°) oven about 30 minutes. While still hot, spread on icing. Cut in slanting pieces to serve.

435. Crumb Cake *(Streuselkuchen)*

Dough:
1 cup milk
1 yeast cake
1 tsp. salt
5 tbls. sugar
4½ cups flour
4 tbls. butter
1 egg

Crumbs:
1 cup hazelnuts, grated
1½ cups flour
¾ cup sugar
1 tsp. cinnamon
1 cup butter, melted

Follow recipe No. 430 exactly to make dough and let rise once. Grease a baking sheet, with an inch high rim, spread dough out on sheet and let it rise once again. Combine hazelnuts, flour, sugar and cinnamon. Add melted butter, drop by drop, while kneading this mixture into crumbs. Rub crumbs between hands to obtain an even distribution and sprinkle over dough. Bake in moderate (350°) oven for 30 minutes.

436. Hazelnut Ring (*Haselnussring*)

2¼ cups flour
1 yeast cake
4 tbls. butter
3 tbls. sugar
salt
1 egg
½ cup milk
1 tsp. lemon juice
1½ cups hazelnuts, roasted
  and chopped
4 tbls. sugar
½ cup sweet cream
1 tbls. vanilla-sugar (sugar
  stored with a vanilla
  bean)
Vanilla Icing (No. 454)

Prepare yeast dough as in No. 430. Beat well and let rise at room temperature. Blend together the roasted finely chopped hazelnuts with sugar, cream and vanilla-sugar. Roll out the dough to finger thickness, spread with the hazelnut mixture, roll together and place in a ring form. Let rise again and bake about a half hour in a hot (400°) oven until nicely browned. Spread with Vanilla Icing while still warm.

437. Nut Crescents (*Nusskipfel*)

Dough:
1 yeast cake
1 scant cup milk
4½ cups flour
1 tsp. salt
7 tbls. butter
5 tbls. sugar
2 eggs

Brushing:
3 tbls. melted butter

Filling:
1½ cups hazelnuts
5 tbls. sugar
2 tbls. water

Vanilla Icing (No. 454)

Dissolve yeast cake in warmed milk. Add other dough ingredients. Knead well. Let dough rise. Roll out ½ inch thick. Cut into triangles or ovals. Brush with melted butter. Prepare filling of hazelnuts, sugar and water. Spread each triangle or oval with this mixture, roll up tight and shape into crescents. Set out on a greased baking sheet. Let rise again. Bake in a hot (400°) oven until nicely browned, 15 to 20 minutes. While still warm, spread with Vanilla Icing.

DEEP FAT BAKING *(Schmalzgebackenes)*

438. Berlin Pancakes, Real Doughnuts *(Berliner Pfannkuchen)*

1 cake yeast
1 cup milk
4 cups flour
3 tbls. butter
2 egg yolks
peel of ½ lemon, grated
pinch of salt
jam or jelly
deep fat
sugar to sprinkle

From yeast, milk and 1 cup of flour, prepare a basic dough (see No. 430). Stir butter and egg yolks to a froth, fold in remaining flour, grated lemon peel and salt. Combine with "rising" dough. Knead thoroughly until large air bubbles form. Let stand in warm place until it rises to twice its original size. Roll out ¼ inch thick and cut out with round cookie cutter. Top half the rounds with jam or jelly and moisten edges with water. Place empty rounds on top and press edges firmly together. Let stand again in warm place to rise. Heat deep fat. Place doughnuts in fat upside down. Brown on both sides. Drain on paper towel. Sprinkle with sugar to serve.
Serves 4.

439. Apple Cookies *(Apfelküchlein)*

5 apples
2 eggs, separated
1¼ cups flour
½ cup milk
2 tbls. sugar
pinch of salt
deep fat
cinnamon and sugar

Pare and core apples and cut in ¼-inch slices. Sprinkle with sugar. Combine egg yolks, flour, milk, sugar and salt and mix smoothly. Fold in beaten egg whites. Dip apple slices in batter and fry in deep fat until golden brown. Sprinkle with cinnamon and sugar.
Serves 2.

440. Rabbits' Ears (*Hasenohren*)

1 egg, whole
2 egg yolks
4 tbls. sugar
2 tbls. cream
1 tsp. rum
flour
fat

Stir eggs and sugar well, add cream, rum and enough flour to form a pliable dough. Roll out rather thin, cut in ribbon-like strips, and roll around a spoon. Drop into hot deep fat until well-browned. Serves 4.

441. Crisp Twists (*Hobelspäne*)

4½ cups flour
1 tsp. baking powder
3 eggs
½ cup sugar
1 tsp. rum
¼ lb. butter
fat
confectioner's sugar

Sift flour and baking powder over a bread board. Mix the eggs, sugar and rum well and combine with flour. Flake chilled butter over and knead all ingredients into dough. Roll dough out thin, cut in strips 4 inches long. Slit one end of each strip, twist strip once and thread twice through slits. Fry in deep fat to a rich golden brown. Drain dry and sprinkle with confectioner's sugar to serve. Serves 4.

442. "Snails" (*Strauben*)

2½ cups flour
1½ cups milk
3 tbls. sugar
4 tbls. butter, melted
3 eggs
pinch of salt
fat
cinnamon and sugar

Knead all ingredients (except fat and cinnamon and sugar) to a soft, smooth dough. Press through a funnel (or pastry-maker) into deep fat, so that pieces of dough curl like snails, snipping off a desired length (about 2 inches). Fry to a golden brown, drain dry on paper towel. Sprinkle with cinnamon and sugar to serve. Serves 4.

CAKES, FROSTINGS AND ICINGS
(Kuchen, Cremefüllen und Glasuren)

443. King's Cake (Königskuchen)

½ lb. butter
5 eggs, separated
1½ cups sugar
½ lemon, juice and grated
   peels
¼ cup rum
1 tsp. salt
¾ cup raisins
2¾ cups flour
1 tbls. cornstarch
½ cup almonds, grated
dash of almond extract
1 tsp. baking powder

Cream butter, stir in egg yolks, sugar, lemon juice and grated peel, rum, salt and raisins. Sift in flour and cornstarch. Fold in grated almonds and almond extract. Stir for about ½ hour (with electric mixer, 10 minutes). Add baking powder and fold in beaten egg whites. Pour into greased cake tin and bake in medium (350°) oven for 1 hour.

444. Marble Cake (Marmorkuchen)

½ lb. butter
4 eggs, separated
1¾ cups sugar
½ tsp. vanilla
4 cups flour
2 tsp. baking powder
1 cup milk
2 squares chocolate
3 tbls. cream or rum
2 tbls. sugar

Cream butter, add egg yolks, sugar and vanilla and stir for 15 minutes. Sift flour and baking powder and add. Add milk and mix well. Fold in stiffly beaten egg whites. Melt chocolate and blend in cream (or rum) and sugar. To one-third of batter add the chocolate mixture. Pour alternating layers of brown and white batter into a greased cake tin. Bake in medium (350°) oven for about 1 hour.

445. Rum Cake
(Rumkuchen "Schwabischer Bund")

¾ lb. butter
5 eggs, separated
1 cup sugar
½ cup almonds, grated
½ lemon, juice and grated
    peel
⅓ cup raisins
1¼ cups flour
1 cup cornstarch
3 tbls. sugar
¾ cup water, hot
3 tbls. rum
Lemon Icing (No. 452)
toasted almonds
candied fruits

Cream butter, add egg yolks and sugar and stir for 30 minutes. Add almonds, lemon juice and peel, raisins, flour and cornstarch. Fold in beaten egg whites. Pour into greased ring-shaped cake tin and bake in medium (350°) oven for 1 hour. Let cool. Dissolve sugar in hot water, add rum and pour into a pan or bowl large enough to hold the finished cake. Set cake in this to soak up rum mixture. Sprinkle top with rum. Top cake with Lemon Icing and decorate with almonds and candied fruits.

446. Apple Cake (Apfelkuchen)

Mellow Dough,
    Sweet (No. 449)
2 lbs. apples
4 tbls. sugar
¼ tsp. cinnamon
½ cup almonds, sliced thin,
    lengthwise
½ cup raisins
butter

Topping:
1 cup sour cream
2 eggs, beaten
½ cup confectioner's sugar

Meringue:
2 egg whites
8 tbls. sugar

Prepare dough and lay out in a greased cake pan (preferably with removable bottom). Peel and core apples and quarter them. Nick surfaces of apples slightly and arrange on top of dough. Sprinkle with sugar, cinnamon, almonds and raisins. Dot with butter. Bake in a hot (425°) oven for 20 minutes. If apples seem dry, cover pan for a short time during baking. May be topped with the mixture of sour cream, eggs and sugar, or with a meringue. Beat egg whites until stiff, fold in sugar and spread over cake shortly before it is done. Replace in oven and bake until the meringue is firm and a light golden brown.

447. Cheese Cake *(Käsekuchen)*

Mellow Dough,
   Sweet (No. 449)
3 cups cottage cheese
1 cup sour cream
1 cup sugar
4 whole eggs
½ lemon, grated peel
¼ tsp. vanilla
1 cup raisins
½ cup cornstarch
1 tsp. flour
1 tsp. baking soda
½ cup almonds, grated

Prepare dough and with it line bottom and sides of a greased cake tin. Strain cottage cheese, stir in cream. Add sugar, eggs, grated lemon peel, vanilla, raisins and cornstarch. Mix flour and baking soda and add. Pour batter into dough lining, top with grated almonds and bake in fairly hot (375°) oven about 1 hour. When done, cool cake in a warm place. Do not chill.

448. Plum Cake *(Pflaumenkuchen)*

Mellow Dough,
   Sweet (No. 449)
2 lbs. plums
½ cup sugar
1 tsp. cinnamon
½ cup almonds, chopped

Prepare dough and line a greased cake tin with it. Pit the plums and arrange in a circle on the dough. Sprinkle with sugar, cinnamon and almonds. Bake in a fairly hot (375°) oven for 30 minutes.

449. Mellow Dough, Sweet *(Mürberteig)*

2 cups flour
¼ lb. butter
½ cup sugar
1 egg
pinch of salt
1 tsp. baking powder

Mix all ingredients and, on a bread board, knead to a supple dough. Roll out and use as instructed in specific recipe. In view of the large butter content of this dough, it should be thoroughly cooled before baking.

450. Mellow Dough, Neutral *(Mürberteig)*

1 cup flour
¼ lb. butter
4 tbls. milk
2 tbls. sugar
pinch of salt
1 tsp. baking powder

Mix all ingredients and, on a bread board, knead to a supple dough. Roll out and use as instructed in specific recipe. In view of the large butter content of this dough, it should be thoroughly cooled before baking.

451. Laminated (Layered) Dough *(Blätterteig)*

2 cups flour
1 cup butter
1 tsp. salt
4 tbls. water

Cool ingredients thoroughly before using. Sift flour onto bread board, separate one-third of the flour and work all but a small piece of the butter into it. Form into a loaf and chill. Make a depression in center of remaining flour and into it add salt, the small piece of butter and, little by little, the water. Work this dough to the consistency of smooth butter until it comes away from board and hands easily. Form into a loaf, slash the top crosswise and chill. Let it stand 5 minutes, then roll out square. Place butter-dough in center of square and roll out both layers together tightly. Fold protruding edges of lower layer over upper layer and roll out again in a thin sheet. Fold this sheet over twice crosswise, so that there are four layers, one on top of another. This completes the first "course." Chill the dough again and let stand 15 minutes. For the second "course," place dough on baking board with open side facing you and roll out, in one direction only, away from you. Roll gently, without excessive pressure. Again fold dough over twice to form four layers. This completes the second "course." Chill dough once more.

In specific recipes, roll completed dough out to required thickness, cut in required shape and place upside down on baking sheet. When instructed to brush with egg yolk or white, be careful it does not run over edges onto baking sheet, as this interferes with proper rising. Always bake in a hot oven. *Note:* Cake bottoms are usually made in 3 or 4 courses, patties in from 4 to 6 courses.

FROSTINGS AND ICINGS

452.   Lemon Icing *(Zitronencreme)*

1 egg
1 cup sugar
2½ tbls. flour
¼ cup lemon juice
grated peels of 2 lemons
1 tbls. butter

Beat egg lightly. Stir in sugar, flour, lemon juice and peel. Melt butter. Add batter and over moderate heat stir until it seethes. Be careful not to let it burn. Chill before using.

453.   Butter Icing *(Buttercreme)*

1 cup butter
3 egg yolks
1 cup confectioner's sugar
½ cup milk

Cream butter, stir in egg yolks and sugar. Scald and chill milk and add, in small dashes, to butter. Beat mixture to a froth.

454.   Vanilla Icing *(Vanillecreme)*

1 cup confectioner's sugar
1 tbls. vanilla-sugar (sugar
    that has been stored
    with vanilla bean)
3 tbls. water

Sift sugar, add vanilla-sugar and water and stir until it becomes thick.

455. Nut Frosting *(Nusscreme)*

2 tbls. cornstarch
1 cup milk
1 cup hazelnuts, grated
4 tbls. sugar
3 tbls. butter
¼ tsp. vanilla
1 cup cream, whipped

Dissolve cornstarch in milk. Add nuts, sugar and butter, and stir over moderate heat until mixture begins to boil. Add vanilla. Let cool. Fold in whipped cream. If stiff frosting is desired, add ½ envelope of gelatine to milk before cooking.

456. Egg-White Icing *(Eiweissglasur)*

1 cup confectioner's sugar
2 egg whites
1 tsp. lemon juice or
  vanilla sugar

Sift sugar into the other ingredients and stir for 15 minutes, or 5 minutes in electric beater. This icing is whiter and spreads better than a sugar icing.

457. Chocolate Frosting *(Schokoladenglasur)*

2 squares chocolate
2 egg whites
1 cup confectioner's sugar

Melt chocolate. Beat egg whites, sift sugar into it and stir for 15 minutes, or 5 minutes in electric beater. Add warm chocolate. If too thin, add extra melted chocolate.

TARTS *(Torten und Törtchen)*

458.   Tart Crust *(Tortenboden)*

3 eggs, separated
1 cup sugar
½ cup milk, hot
¼ lemon, juice and grated
  peels
4 tbls. butter
1 cup flour
¼ tsp. salt
1½ tbls. baking powder

Beat egg yolks and add ½ cup sugar gradually, beating to a froth. Mix milk with remaining sugar, lemon juice and peel and butter. Sift together the flour, salt and baking powder and combine all mixtures. Fold in beaten egg whites. Grease a pan and sprinkle it with flour. Bake in a moderate (350°) oven for 35 minutes. When cool, slice twice horizontally, spread layers with cream of your choice and set back together.

459.   Chocolate Tart *(Schokoladetorte)*

½ lb. butter
5 eggs
1½ cups sugar
4½ cups flour
½ cup cocoa or 2 squares
  chocolate
1½ cups water, warm
1½ tsp. baking powder
Chocolate Frosting
  (No. 457)
Small Chocolate Caps
  (No. 498)

Cream butter. Beat eggs in a warm place. Gradually add sugar, eggs and most of the flour to the butter. Dissolve cocoa or chocolate in water and add to batter. Stir for ½ hour (electric mixer, 5 to 10 minutes). Sift remaining flour and baking powder into mixture and blend well. Pour into a greased cake tin and bake in hot (400°) oven for 1 hour. Let cool, then decorate with Chocolate Frosting and Chocolate Caps.

460. Hazelnut Tart *(Haselnusstorte)*

5 eggs, separated
¾ cup sugar
6 tbls. water
1 cup chopped hazelnuts
1½ cups flour
1 tsp. baking powder
Vanilla Icing (No. 454)
whole shelled hazelnuts, or
　1 cup cream, whipped,
　¼ cup nuts, grated

Beat egg yolks, sugar and water to a thick batter. Fold in nuts. Sift in flour and baking powder and fold in beaten egg whites. Pour into a greased cake tin and bake in medium (375°) oven for 30 to 40 minutes. Spread on Vanilla Icing and decorate with whole hazelnuts. This may be varied by slicing the tart twice and filling layers with Nut Frosting (No. 455) or with whipped cream and grated nuts.

461. Macaroon Tart *(Makronentorte)*

1 lb. almonds, grated
2 cups sugar
8 egg whites
1 lemon, juice and grated
　peel
Mellow Dough,
　Sweet (No. 449)
candied fruit or jelly

Combine grated almonds, sugar, 2 egg whites, lemon peel and juice and stir over very low heat until lukewarm. Let it cool. Prepare dough, roll out ½ inch thick and lay in greased cake tin. Pierce bottom with a fork (for ventilation). Bake in hot (400°) oven until half done (about 10 minutes). Beat remaining egg whites until stiff and fold into almond mixture. Spread over tart crust. Replace in oven and bake until a pleasant light yellow, about 10 minutes. Decorate with candied fruit or sweet jelly.

462. Chocolate and Nut Tart (Schokoladen-Nusstorte)

⅓ cup butter
1⅔ cups brown sugar
3 eggs, separated
1½ cups milk
2 cups flour
1 tsp. baking powder
7 squares chocolate
1½ cups walnuts, grated
1 tsp. grated lemon peel
½ tsp. vanilla
Chocolate Frosting (No. 457)
or Vanilla Icing (No. 454)

Cream butter, stir in 1 cup sugar. Add 2 beaten egg yolks and ½ cup milk. Sift in flour and baking powder. Fold in beaten egg whites. Melt chocolate in double boiler, add ⅔ cup sugar, 1 cup milk and 1 egg yolk. Stir well. Let cool and combine with first batter. Stir in nuts, lemon peel and vanilla. Grease loaf pan, sprinkle with flour and pour in batter. Bake in moderately hot (385°) oven for 35 minutes. Turn out of pan and spread with either icing.

463. Almond Tart (Mandeltorte)

3 tbls. butter
6 tbls. confectioner's sugar
4 eggs
1 jigger cherry brandy
2 tbls. cornstarch
1 cup almonds, grated
dash of almond extract
1 cup cream, whipped

Cream butter, stir in sugar, eggs and cherry brandy. Add cornstarch and almonds and almond extract and blend well. Butter a cake tin (or muffin tin) and line with wax paper. Pour in batter and bake in a hot (375°) oven for 25 minutes. Lift out on paper and let cool. Before serving, decorate with whipped cream.

464. Nougat Tart *(Nougattorte)*

3 eggs, separated
1¾ cups confectioner's sugar
½ tsp. vanilla
5 tbls. water
1½ cups flour
½ tsp. baking powder
¾ cup cornstarch
3 tbls. chocolate, grated
⅓ cup butter
2 whole eggs
1 egg yolk
⅓ cup sugar
½ tsp. vanilla
½ cup cholocate, grated
½ cup almonds, toasted
     and grated
⅔ cup shortening
Chocolate Frosting (No. 457)
almond halves

Beat egg yolks, sugar, vanilla and water to a froth. Sift in flour, baking powder and cornstarch. Add grated chocolate and stir into batter. Melt butter, let cool and add. Fold in beaten egg whites. Pour into a well-greased pan and bake 45 minutes in medium-hot (375°) oven. Let cool and cut in 3 slices. For cream filling, stir eggs, egg yolk, sugar and vanilla to a froth. Add grated chocolate and toasted, grated almonds, by spoonfuls. Melt shortening and let cool to hand temperature. Add very slowly to mixture. Heap filling on slices of tart. Replace slices, one on top of the other. Frost and decorate with almond halves.

465. Mocha (or Coffee) Cream Tart *(Mokkacremetorte)*

Tart Crust (No. 458)
3 tbls. coffee
1 cup water, boiling
1 cup sweet cream
4 egg yolks
½ cup sugar
1 cup butter
chocolate chips

Prepare tart crust, let it cool, then slice in thirds. Scald coffee in boiling water and let stand for 10 minutes for penetration. Strain, stir into cream. Combine egg yolks, sugar and coffee-cream mixture in double boiler and cook, stirring constantly, until thick. Let cool. Cream butter and stir into mixture. Spread cream generously on tart slices; replace slices one on top of another. Spread cream also over entire outside of tart. Decorate top with any remaining cream, garnish with chocolate chips. This recipe may be varied by using lemon, orange or any other fruit flavor instead of coffee.

466. Windbags (Cream Puffs) (*Windbeutel*)

1 cup water
½ cup butter
1 tbls. sugar
pinch of salt
1 cup flour
4 eggs
1 cup, or more,
    whipped cream

Combine water, butter, sugar and salt over low heat. When boiling point is reached, add flour (all at once). Stir and form into a firm dough. Remove from heat and, one by one, beat in eggs and stir to a smooth batter. Scoop by tablespoonfuls onto a greased baking sheet, forming tight and somewhat high mounds. 2 inches apart. Bake 15 minutes in a hot (425°) oven. Reduce heat to 350° and bake 15 to 20 minutes longer. Be sure they are thoroughly baked or they will collapse. Cool, cut a slit in one side, into which put whipped cream.

467. Apple Tartlets (*Gefüllte Krapfen*)

6-8 apples
¼ cup wine
1 tbls. sugar
Laminated Dough
    (No. 451)
1 egg, separated

Peel, core and slice apples and stew in wine and sugar until soft, but not too soft. Prepare dough in four layers and roll out thin. Cut out with round cookie cutter. Brush edges, carefully, with egg white. Spread with apples (or with cherries, similarly prepared, marmalade, or a nut filling). Fold over in half and notch the edges. Or dough may be cut in squares, spread with desired filling and then caught up at the corners and pressed together in the center. Brush with egg yolk and bake in moderately hot (375°) oven until brown, about 15 minutes.

CHRISTMAS CAKES AND CANDIES
(Weihnachtsgebäck und Konfekt)

CAKES

468.　Honey Spice Cake (Honiglebkuchen)

2 eggs
¾ cup sugar
1 tsp. cinnamon
pinch of cloves, ground
¼ cup candied orange or
　　lemon peel, chopped
2 tbls. rum
4 cups flour
¾ cup honey
1 cup almonds, chopped
1 tsp. baking powder
Egg-White Icing (No. 456)
　　or Chocolate Frosting
　　(No. 457)

Stir eggs and sugar to a froth, add spices, candied peel, rum and one cup of the flour. Mix honey and almonds and stir in another cup of flour. Combine egg dough and honey dough and knead together on a floured baking board. Mix baking powder with remaining flour and knead into dough. Roll out ½ inch thick and cut out desired shapes with cookie cutters. Grease baking sheet and set out cookies, leaving ½ inch between them. Bake in hot (400°) oven 10 to 12 minutes. Brush cookies while still hot with Egg-White Icing or, when cool, with Chocolate Frosting.

469.　Simple Spice Cake (Einfache Lebkuchen)

1½ cups honey
5 cups flour
½ cup almonds, chopped
1 tsp. cinnamon
pinch of cloves, ground
¼ cup candied orange or
　　lemon peel, chopped
¼ tsp. baking powder
Egg-White Icing (No. 456)

Warm but do not cook the honey. Add all other ingredients (except icing) and knead to a smooth dough. Roll dough out evenly ½ inch thick and bake on a buttered baking sheet in a moderate oven (350°) until brown, about 20 minutes. While still hot, spread on icing and cut into squares.

470. Nut Spice Cake (*Nusslebkuchen*)

2 cups shelled almonds,
  hazelnuts or walnuts
4 eggs
1¾ cups sugar
1 tbls. vanilla-sugar (sugar
  stored with a vanilla
  bean)
1 cup flour, scant
pinch of baking powder
wafers (oblaten)
Chocolate Frosting
  (No. 457)

Chop nuts coarsely. Stir eggs and sugar to a froth and mix in nuts. Stir in flour and baking powder. Spread mixture on wafers (oblaten) and let dry overnight. Next day bake in slow (300°) oven until brown, about 20 to 30 minutes, keeping door slightly ajar. Top with Chocolate Frosting.

Note: Oblaten may be bought at fine grocery shops and department stores.

471. Nürnberger Spice Cake (*Nürnberger Lebkuchen*)

5 eggs
2¼ cups sugar
1 tbls. cinnamon
pinch of cloves, ground
pinch of nutmeg
¼ cup candied orange and
  lemon peel, chopped
3 cups almonds, chopped
1 cup flour, scant
pinch of baking powder
wafers (oblaten)
Egg-White Icing (No. 456)
  or Chocolate Frosting
  (No. 457)
confectioner's sugar

Stir eggs and sugar until smooth and thick. One after another add and mix in other ingredients through baking powder. Spread ½ inch thick on oblaten and let stand overnight to dry. Next day, bake in slow (300°) oven, leaving door slightly ajar, for 20 to 30 minutes. Top with icing while still hot, or with frosting when cool. Just before serving, sprinkle with confectioner's sugar.

472. Peppernuts *(Pfeffernusse)*

3 eggs
1 generous cup sugar
⅓ cup almonds
⅓ cup candied orange and
   lemon peel
1 tsp. cinnamon
dash of cloves, ground
dash of pepper
dash of baking powder
3 cups flour
sugar, vanilla-sugar or Egg-
   White Icing (No. 456)

Stir eggs and sugar until frothy. Blanch and grind almonds. Chop lemon and orange peel finely. Mix these and all other ingredients through flour together and knead into a dough. Roll out ½ inch thick on a floured board and cut with biscuit cutter to about size and shape of a 50¢-piece. Butter a baking sheet and set cookies on it overnight to dry. Next day bake in slow (300°) degree oven until brown, about 20 to 30 minutes. Frost with plain or vanilla-flavored white sugar or with icing.

473. Hazelnut Macaroons *(Haselnussmakronen)*

2 egg whites
1 cup confectioner's sugar
1 cup hazelnuts, mashed
1 tbls. lemon juice
25 whole hazlenuts

Beat egg whites until stiff. Stir in confectioner's sugar, hazelnuts and lemon juice. Using two teaspoons, scoop out macaroons from dough and place on buttered baking sheet. Top each one with a whole hazelnut. Let stand overnight to dry. Bake in moderate (350°) oven 15 to 20 minutes.

474. Almond Macaroons *(Mandelmakronen)*

2 egg whites
¾ cup sugar
1 tsp. lemon juice
¾ cup almonds, grated

Beat egg whites until stiff. Add sugar, lemon juice and almonds. The mixture should be quite firm; if necessary, add more almonds. With two teaspoons scoop up macaroons from dough. Set out on buttered baking sheet and let dry for several hours. Bake in moderate (350°) oven 15 to 20 minutes.

475. Coconut Macaroons *(Kokonussmakronen)*

3 egg whites
½ cup sugar
1 tbls. lemon juice
1 cup shredded coconut
2 tbls. sweetened condensed milk
wafers (oblaten)

Beat egg whites until stiff. Add sugar and lemon juice. Stir in shredded coconut and condensed milk. Using two teaspoons, scoop out macaroons and set on buttered baking sheet (or wafers). Allow to dry several hours and bake in moderate (350°) oven 15 to 20 minutes.

476. Cinnamon Stars *(Zimtsterne)*

2 egg whites
1 cup confectioner's sugar
1 tsp. cinnamon
¾ cup almonds, grated
coarse sugar

Beat egg whites until stiff. Add confectioner's sugar and stir well. Set aside ½ cup of this for icing. Stir cinnamon and grated almonds into remaining batter and knead thoroughly. Sprinkle baking board with extra coarse grained sugar and roll dough out ½ inch thick. Cut out star-shaped cookies. Let dry for several hours. Brush with the set-aside icing and bake in moderate (350°) oven, 8 to 10 minutes, until brown.

477. Oat Macaroons *(Haferflockenmakronen)*

5 tbls. butter
1 cup sugar
½ cup almonds, shredded
dash of almond extract
2 tbls. cocoa
2 cups quick oats
¼ cup milk
2 cups flour
1 tsp. baking powder

Cream butter and gradually add and blend in sugar and other ingredients. Scoop out macaroons. Set out on a buttered baking sheet and bake 15 to 20 minutes in moderate (350°) oven.

478. Hazelnut Strips *(Haselnussschnitten)*

2 egg whites
1 cup confectioner's sugar, sifted
1 tsp. lemon juice
1 cup hazelnuts, grated
coarse sugar

Beat egg whites until stiff, stir in sugar and lemon juice. Put aside ½ cup of this mixture for icing. To the rest add hazelnuts and knead into dough. Sprinkle a board with coarse sugar and roll out dough ½ inch thick. Cut in 2-inch strips. Place on buttered baking sheet and let stand to dry for several hours. Brush on icing previously put aside. Bake in moderate (350°) oven about 15 minutes.

479. Almond Rainbows *(Mandelbögen)*

¼ cup almonds, grated
¼ cup almonds, shredded
1 cup sugar
3 egg whites
1 tsp. cinnamon
peel of ½ lemon, chopped
1 tbls. lemon juice
1 tbls. candied lemon peel, chopped
wafers (oblaten)

Toast the almonds and sugar over low heat to a golden brown. Beat egg whites until stiff. Fold in all other ingredients. Spread mixture thinly on wafers and bake in slow (300°) oven until golden brown. Cut in thin strips while still hot and bend over a rolling pin to form rainbows.

480. Almond Half-Moons *(Mandelhalbmonde)*

2 egg whites
1 cup confectioner's sugar
1 tsp. lemon juice
¼ cup almonds, grated
coarse sugar

Beat egg whites until stiff, then stir in sugar and lemon juice. Put aside ½ cup for icing. To remaining mixture, add grated almonds. Sprinkle baking board with coarse sugar and roll out dough ¼ inch thick. Cut crescents with cookie cutter. Set aside, on wax paper, to dry several hours. Brush with icing previously set aside and bake in moderate (350°) oven until golden brown.

481. Chocolate Shells *(Schokolademuscheln)*

2 egg whites
¼ cup sugar
3 squares chocolate
⅜ cup almonds, grated
¼ tsp. cinnamon
¼ tsp. cloves, ground
coarse sugar, to turn in

Beat egg whites until stiff and stir in sugar. Melt chocolate and add, together with almonds, cinnamon and cloves. Shape into small balls, turn in sugar, then press with thumb to resemble seashells. Place on wax paper to dry several hours, then bake in slow (300°) oven until golden brown, 20 to 30 minutes.

482. Urchins *(Spitzbuben)*

2 cups flour
⅔ cup butter
1 cup sugar
½ cup almonds, chopped
currant jelly or raspberry
jam
vanilla-sugar (sugar stored
with a vanilla bean)

Work flour, butter, sugar and almonds together on a baking board into a smooth mellow dough, and chill. Roll out thin, cut with cookie cutter and bake in moderate (350°) oven until golden brown. Let cool. Spread with jam or jelly. Place one on top of another, like a sandwich. Sprinkle with vanilla-flavored sugar.

483. Raspberry Mounds *(Himbeerbrötchen)*

2 eggs
1 cup sugar
2 tbls. raspberry jam
1 generous cup flour

Stir eggs and sugar to a froth. Add raspberry jam and flour and blend well. Shape into mounds. Let dry overnight on wax paper, then bake in moderate (350°) oven until golden brown, about 10 to 15 minutes.

484. Mellow Cookies *("Heidesand")*

½ cup butter
¾ cup sugar
1¼ cups flour
2 tbls. vanilla-sugar (sugar
    stored with a vanilla
    bean)
1 tsp. baking powder
pinch of baking soda

Melt butter and let brown slightly. Stir in other ingredients. Shape dough into little round balls, set on wax paper to dry several hours, then bake in fairly hot (400°) oven until golden brown, about 20 minutes.

485. Vanilla Kisses *(Vanillebusserln)*

1¼ cups sugar
6 eggs
2 tbls. vanilla-sugar (sugar
    stored with a vanilla
    bean
3½ cups flour

Beat sugar, eggs and vanilla-sugar for 45 minutes (in electric mixer, 10 to 15 minutes), gradually adding flour, a tablespoon at a time. Shape dough into little mounds, place on greased baking sheet overnight to dry. Bake in slow (300°) oven until brown, about 30 minutes.

486. Cornmeal Mounds *(Maisgebäck)*

5 tbls. butter
2 eggs
1 cup sugar
dash of almond extract
juice of ½ lemon
peel of ½ lemon, grated
2 cups flour
3 cups cornmeal
1½ tsp. baking powder
2 cups milk

Cream butter, add eggs, sugar and flavorings. Stir well. Sift flour, cornmeal and baking powder into the milk and fold into batter. Butter baking sheet, shape dough into mounds, and bake in fairly hot (400°) oven until brown, about 30 minutes.

487. Butter "S"

2 cups flour
½ cup butter
3 egg yolks
⅓ cup sugar
peel of ½ lemon, grated
1 egg white, beaten
coarse sugar

Sprinkle baking board with flour and mix all ingredients (except egg white and coarse sugar) and work quickly into dough. Let stand 30 minutes in a cool place. Roll out ½ inch thick, cut in even strips and bend strips to resemble letter "S." Set on greased baking sheet in a cool place another 30 minutes. Brush tops with beaten egg white, sprinkle with coarse-grained sugar and bake in fairly hot (400°) oven, about 20 minutes.

488. Raisin Rolls (*Rosinenbrötchen*)

4 eggs
1¼ cups sugar
½ cup raisins, chopped
3 cups flour

Stir eggs and sugar to a froth. Fold in raisins and sift in flour. Butter baking sheet, scoop out small mounds of dough, place on baking sheet and let stand overnight to dry. Bake in a moderate (350°) oven until brown, about 10 to 15 minutes.

489. Orange or Lemon Rolls (*Pomeranzenbrötchen*)

4 eggs
1¼ cups sugar
⅓ cup candied orange or
    lemon peel, chopped
3 cups flour

Stir eggs and sugar to a froth. Fold in orange or lemon peel. Sift in flour. Butter baking sheet, scoop out small mounds, place on baking sheet and let stand overnight to dry. Bake in moderate (350°) oven until brown, 10 to 15 minutes.

490. Christmas Stollen
(*Weihnachts—oder Sächsischer Stollen*)

8 cups flour, sifted
1½ cups milk, lukewarm
2 yeast cakes
1 tbls. salt
1 cup sugar
1 cup butter
1¼ cups raisins
1½ cups almonds, grated
½ cup candied lemon or
    orange peel, chopped
2 tbls. butter
vanilla-sugar (sugar stored
    with a vanilla bean) and
    confectioner's sugar, or Egg-
    White Icing (No. 456)

Prepare a firm yeast dough (see No. 430) of flour, milk, yeast, salt, sugar and butter, and work it until it blisters. Knead in raisins, grated almonds and candied peel. Cover dough and let it rise to twice its size. Sprinkle bread board with flour and roll dough out into an oval, about 1 inch thick. Fold in half, letting lower layer protrude. Place on greased baking sheet and again let rise in a warm, draft-free place. Brush with melted butter. Bake in fairly hot (400°) oven until done, 45 to 60 minutes. Brush with butter again while still hot. Mix confectioner's and vanilla-sugar and sprinkle on loaf or use icing.

491. Fruit Loaf (*Schnitz—oder Hutzelbrot*)

2 lbs. dried prunes
2 lbs. dried pears
½ lb. walnuts, shelled
½ lb. hazelnuts or almonds
¼ lb. candied orange or
    lemon peel
¼ lb. figs
1 cup milk
2 yeast cakes
12 cups flour
1 tsp. cinnamon
pinch of cloves, ground
1 tbls. salt
1 tsp. anise extract
slivered almonds
whole walnuts
candied peel

Soak whole dried fruits in water overnight. Remove, saving water. Remove prune pits, chop all fruit and cook in same water for 30 minutes. Chop nuts coarsely and cut orange peel and figs in small cubes. Mix milk, yeast and flour to a dough and beat hard, until it blisters and comes easily off hands and bowl. Now work in all fruits, nuts, peels, spices and extract of anise, being careful not to crush the fruit unduly. Sprinkle lightly with flour, cover and set in warm place until it rises double its size. Shape dough into loaves, decorate with slivered almonds, whole walnuts and candied peel. Let rise again, then bake in fairly hot (400°) oven until thoroughly brown, 45 to 60 minutes.

CANDIES

492. Marzipan

1½ cups almonds, grated
1½ cups confectioner's sugar
dash of almond extract
1 cup sweet chocolate,
    grated

Grate almonds very fine, twice if necessary. Mix with sugar and almond extract and heat slightly. Cool and add a little extra sugar if necessary to knead into a dough. Cover dough tightly and let stand overnight. Shape into small balls, and tumble in grated chocolate.

493. Nut Brittle *(Krokant)*

¼ lb. almonds, peanuts, or
    other nuts
1 tsp. vanilla-sugar (sugar
    stored with a vanilla
    bean)
1⅔ cups sugar

Chop nuts coarsely and mix with vanilla-sugar. Melt sugar in large skillet, over low heat, add almonds and fry to a golden brown. Grease baking sheet and rolling pin. Spread mixture on sheet, roll out with pin. Cut in squares while still hot. Store in a closed metal box.

494. Sugar Almonds *(Gebrannte Mandeln)*

¾ cups sugar
4 tbls. water
¾ cup almonds, whole,
    shelled
¼ tsp. cinnamon

Cook sugar and water until thick and syrupy. Remove from heat and add almonds. Stir until sugar crackles. Heat and repeat melting and hardening process twice. Sprinkle with cinnamon. When cinnamon dissolves, pour mixture out on greased baking sheet and separate with two forks.

495.   Peanut Candy *(Erdnusskonfekt)*

1 tbls. butter
2 cups brown sugar
⅓ cup cream
¼ tsp. vanilla
¼ tsp. salt
¾ cup peanuts, chopped

Melt butter in large skillet, add sugar and cream and bring to a boil. Continue cooking until a small sample dropped in cold water forms a firm ball. Add vanilla. Remove from heat and beat to a froth. Sprinkle nuts with salt and stir into mixture. Spread out on a buttered baking sheet and cut in squares. Walnuts and coconut may be prepared in the same way, but with coconut, reduce vanilla by half.

496.   French Nougats *(Französischer Nougat)*

1½ cups sugar
1¼ cups almonds, chopped
2 squares bitter chocolate

Stir sugar over low heat until melted. Add almonds, mix in, then pour out on greased surface. Keep working with spatula to prevent premature hardening. Cut in four sections and roll each part up until it is 1 inch thick. Cut in pieces 1½ inches long. Melt chocolate in double boiler. Stir it well, remove from heat and cool. Dip nougat pieces in chocolate and set out on wax paper to dry.

497.   Chocolate Truffles *(Schokoladetrüffel)*

¼ cup butter
½ cup chocolate, grated
1 tbls. rum
¼ cup chocolate crumbs

Cream butter, add chocolate and rum. Chill and let stand. When cold, form small balls, tumble in coarsely grated chocolate (crumbs) and set out in fancy paper forms to dry.

498. Small Chocolate Caps (*Schokoladehütchen*)

1 egg white
1 tsp. vanilla-sugar (sugar stored with a vanilla bean)
1 tsp. liqueur or 2 tbls. coffee extract
½ cup confectioner's sugar
1 tbls. shortening
½ cup cocoa, powdered

Beat egg white until stiff. Add flavorings and enough confectioner's sugar to make a paste that can be formed into little balls. Set out overnight in a cool place to dry. Melt shortening, stir in cocoa and sweeten with confectioner's sugar to taste. Lift balls with toothpicks and dip into chocolate.

499. Nut Fondant (*Fondantnüsse*)

1 egg white
½ tbls. water
½ tsp. vanilla or coffee extract
confectioner's sugar
walnuts, shelled and halved, or dates, pitted and halved

Stir white of egg and water until frothy. Add vanilla or coffee extract. Little by little add confectioner's sugar (about 2 cups) until mixture can be shaped into small balls. Sandwich each ball between two halves of a walnut or date. Top dates with walnut halves. Let dry and place in fancy paper cups to serve.

500. Coconut Bonbons (*Kokosnussbonbons*)

2 tsp. butter
1½ cups sugar
½ cup milk
⅓ cup shredded coconut
½ tsp. vanilla

Melt butter in skillet. Add sugar and milk and stir until sugar dissolves completely. Bring to a boil and cook for 12 minutes. Remove from heat and stir in coconut and vanilla. Beat until edges of mixture start to harden. Butter a baking sheet and pour out candy. Cool and cut in squares. A half cup of shredded nuts may be substituted for the coconut.

501.   Vanilla Caramels *(Vanillekaramellen)*

¼ cup butter
⅔ cup milk
2⅔ cup sugar
1 tsp. vanilla

Melt butter in skillet. Add milk and sugar and cook until mixture will form small firm ball when dropped into cold water. Remove from heat, add vanilla and beat to a froth. Pour out on buttered baking sheet and, when cold, cut in squares.

502.   Candied Orange Peel
(Kandierte-Orangenschalen)

4 oranges
½ cup sugar
½ cup water
coarse sugar

Select thin-skinned oranges. Remove peel in quarters, cover with cold water and cook until tender. Drain. Remove inner white linings and cut orange peel with scissors into thin strips. Cook sugar and water until it spins a thread when spoon is raised. Then add peel and cook together for 5 minutes. Remove strips, sprinkle with coarse-grained sugar and let dry.

503.   Quince Candy *(Quittenkonfekt)*

3 cups quince pulp
3 cups sugar

Cut up about 2 pounds of quinces and cook in small amount of water until tender. Cool, covered. Mash through strainer and combine with sugar. Let simmer over low heat until liquid thickens. Pour out ½ inch thick. Chill, then cut in any desired shape. Tumble in sugar. To store, use wax paper between layers.

INDEX

Index

205